MAR   2018

Tracking Serial Killers

How to Catch a Murderer

By Christine Honders

Portions of this book originally appeared in
Tracking Serial Killers by Diane Yancey.

LUCENT PRESS

Published in 2018 by
Lucent Press, an Imprint of Greenhaven Publishing, LLC
353 3rd Avenue
Suite 255
New York, NY 10010

Designer: Deanna Paternostro
Editor: Vanessa Oswald

Library of Congress Cataloging-in-Publication Data

Names: Honders, Christine.
Title: Tracking serial killers: how to catch a murderer / Christine Honders.
Description: New York : Lucent Press, 2018. | Series: Crime scene investigations | Includes index.
Identifiers: ISBN 9781534560895 (library bound) | ISBN 9781534560901 (ebook)
Subjects: LCSH: Serial murder investigation–United States–Juvenile literature. | Serial murderers–United States–Psychology–Juvenile literature. | Criminal behavior, Prediction of–United States–Juvenile literature.
Classification: LCC HV8079.H6 Y35 2018 | DDC 363.25'9523–dc23

Printed in the United States of America

CPSIA compliance information: Batch #BS17KL: For further information contact Greenhaven Publishing LLC, New York, New York at 1-844-317-7404.

Please visit our website, www.greenhavenpublishing.com. For a free color catalog of all our high-quality books, call toll free 1-844-317-7404 or fax 1-844-317-7405.

Contents

Foreword

For decades, popular television programs and movies have depicted the life and work of police officers, detectives, and crime scene investigators. Many of these shows and films portray forensic scientists as the brains responsible for cracking cases and bringing criminals to justice. Undoubtedly, these crime scene analysts are an important part in the process of crime solving. With modern technology and advances in forensic analysis, these highly trained experts are a crucial component of law enforcement systems all across the world.

Police officers and detectives are also integral members of the law enforcement team. They are the ones who respond to 911 calls about crime, collect physical evidence, and use their high level of training to identify suspects and culprits. They work right alongside forensic investigators to figure out the mysteries behind why a crime is committed, and the entire team cooperates to gather enough evidence to convict someone in a court of law.

Ever since the first laws were recorded, crime scene investigation has been handled in roughly the same way. An authority is informed that a crime has been committed; someone looks around the crime scene and interviews potential witnesses; suspects are identified based on evidence and testimony; and, finally, someone is formally accused of committing a crime. This basic plan is generally effective, and criminals are often caught and brought to justice. Throughout history, however, certain limitations have sometimes prevented authorities from finding out who was responsible for a crime.

There are many reasons why a crime goes unsolved: Maybe a dead body was found too late, evidence was tampered with, or witnesses lied. Sometimes, even the greatest technology of the age is simply not good enough to process and analyze the evidence at a crime scene. In the United States during the 20th century, for example, the person responsible for the infamous Zodiac killings was never found, despite the earnest efforts of hundreds of policemen, detectives, and forensic analysts.

In modern times, science and technology are integral to the investigative process. From DNA analysis to high-definition surveillance video, it has become much more difficult to commit a crime and get away with it. Using advanced computers and immense databases, microscopic skin cells from a crime scene can be collected and then analyzed by a forensic scientist, leading detectives to the home of the culprit of a crime. Dozens of people work behind the scenes of criminal investigations to figure out the unique and complex elements of a crime. Although this process is still time-consuming and complicated, technology is constantly improving and adapting to the needs of police forces worldwide.

This series is designed to help young readers understand the systems in place to allow forensic professionals to do their jobs. Covering a wide range of topics, from the assassination of President John F. Kennedy to 21st-century cybercriminals, these titles describe in detail the ways in which technology and criminal investigations have evolved over more than 50 years. They cite eyewitnesses and experts in order to give a detailed and nuanced picture of the difficult task of rooting out criminals. Although television shows and movies add drama to the crime scene investigation process, these real-life stories have enough drama on their own. This series sticks to the facts surrounding some of the highest-profile criminal cases of the modern era and the people who work to solve them and other crimes every day.

Introduction
The Killers Next Door

In 2005 in Wichita, Kansas, a man named Dennis Rader, former Cub Scout leader and active member of his church, was working as a city compliance supervisor. He appeared to everyone to be a regular guy. Maybe he was a bit overzealous in being a stickler for the rules, such as measuring the length of people's grass and getting a little too much enjoyment from the limited authority he had over the local residents, but the married father of two was described by many as friendly and pleasant.

At the same time, the Wichita police were trying to find a serial killer, one who—from 1974 until 1991—caused the citizens of the city to live in fear. He called himself the BTK (Bind, Torture, and Kill) Killer and would break into people's homes, cut their phone lines, and murder them in slow, torturous ways. Between 1977 and 1978, the first thing the women in Wichita did when they got home was check their phone

for a dial tone. For years he not only got away with these murders, but also would write letters, leave packages, and make phone calls to the media and the police, taunting them. The BTK Killer had not struck since 1991, but in 2004, when the media began reporting on the 30th anniversary of his crimes, he sent letters, a photo of one of the victims, a word puzzle, and even an outline for the "BTK Story" to the police. These communications finally led authorities to the identification and arrest of Dennis Rader. The community was stunned that a quiet, normal-looking man could have committed such heinous acts.

Rader pled guilty and opened up during the trial about his crimes, explaining how he researched and selected each murder, which he called "projects," up to the grisly details of each victim's final moments. When speaking about the murder of Shirley Vian, who he strangled to death while her three children were locked in a bathroom, he said he

Author Katherine Ramsland described how Dennis Rader, shown here, separated his normal life from his life as the BTK Killer. He called the serial killer part of his personality "the Minotaur."

would have killed the children as well if their phone had not rung, causing him to flee. Rader said in court, "I probably would have hung the little girl. Like I said, I'm pretty mean or could be. But on the other hand, I'm very—you know, I'm a nice guy."[1]

Murderers Throughout Time

Although Dennis Rader gained widespread notoriety for his crimes, he was not the first killer to take the lives of multiple victims in the United States.

In the early 1800s, Samuel Green rampaged through New England, sexually assaulting, stealing, and murdering until he was arrested and hanged in 1822 in Boston, Massachusetts. In 1893, Herman Webster Mudgett, also known as H.H. Holmes, trapped, tortured, and murdered women who stayed as guests at the Chicago hotel he had opened for the World's Columbian Exposition. In 1895, he confessed to 27 murders in Chicago, Illinois; Indianapolis, Indiana; and Toronto, Canada, but officials

HERMAN WEBSTER MUDGETT *alias* H. H. HOLMES.

H.H. Holmes built his "murder castle," which contained many small rooms with trapdoors and gas jets, so he could torture, kill, and dispose of his victims.

believe he may have murdered between 130 and 200 people.

Other notorious American serial killers include Albert Fish, who was known to eat his victims after killing them, and Edmund Kemper, who killed his grandparents and six female hitchhikers in California before murdering his mother and her friend in 1973. Jeffrey Dahmer was convicted in 1992 for sexually assaulting, murdering, dismembering, and eating some of his 17 victims. Aileen Wuornos took the lives of at least seven men in 1989 and 1990 and was considered a rare case because most serial killers are male.

Male or female, serial killers are not limited to the United States. A Roman woman named Locusta poisoned ancient Romans during the first century AD. Jack the Ripper murdered and mutilated at least five sex workers (who are also sometimes known as prostitutes) in London in 1888. Former Russian police officer Mikhail Popkov killed at least 24 women between 1992 and 2000. Nicknamed "the Werewolf," he targeted women that reportedly looked like his mother.

"The Dog Made Me Do It"

The fact that Popkov, Rader, and others were able to evade authorities for years emphasizes the difficulty law enforcement officials have identifying and catching serial killers. They are much better at labeling and defining them. By definition, serial killers are men or women who have taken the lives of at least two victims in a series of separate events. Their victims are typically vulnerable strangers, such as young women whom they can control. Sex workers are popular targets because many of them are runaways with no families.

There are different motivations for serial killers, but they generally fall into one of four categories: the thrill, the sense of power, financial gain, or to rid the world of what the killer thinks is evil. They kill when they are feeling stressed, and with the murder comes a sense of relief. However, the relief is generally only temporary, which is why they feel the urge to kill again.

Experts point to childhood abuse as a factor. Edmund Kemper, for instance, was shamed and humiliated by his domineering mother, and Aileen Wuornos was abused as a child. Others point to physical or mental factors. Schizophrenia, a mental illness that can cause hallucinations, delusions, and paranoia, is the most common mental illness among serial killers. David Berkowitz, or the Son of Sam, killed six people in the 1970s and said the neighbor's dog told him to do it. He was diagnosed with paranoid schizophrenia. A 2014 study in Glasgow, Scotland, found similar traits among different murderers. It showed

Serial Killer Frequency by Decade (Decade of First Kill)

Decade	U.S.	International	Total
1900	49	23	72
1910	52	23	75
1920	62	41	103
1930	55	31	86
1940	55	45	100
1950	72	41	113
1960	217	76	293
1970	605	160	765
1980	768	217	985
1990	669	322	991
2000	371	295	666
2010	117	113	230

Mike Aamodt, "Serial Killer Statistics," Radford University, September 4, 2016. maamodt.asp.radford.edu/Serial%20Killer%20Information%20Center/Serial%20Killer%20Statistics.pdf.

that people with autism who have also suffered a head injury and are triggered by psychosocial stress, such as child abuse, are more likely to commit serial killing.

Whether serial killers are born or created, their numbers are on the decline. From the 1920s to the 1950s, multiple murders were rare in the United States. Serial killing increased sharply in the 1970s—65 percent higher than in the previous decade. It reached its peak in the United States during the 1980s, with 768 serial killings. However, in the 2000s, the number of serial killings per decade had dropped by half, and by 2010, it dropped another 50 percent to 117. Some explanations for this include the advancement of technology. Better record keeping and fingerprint databases help police find killers. DNA forensic testing has made it easier to identify serial killers, and everyone has cell phones and cameras, which makes it harder to get away with crime.

Planning and Persistence

No matter what factors cause serial killers to kill, everyone agrees that they are difficult to catch. They are organized and plan, stalk, and think about how they can carry out their crime without leaving physical evidence. They use gloves, chemicals, and masks, and they carefully clean up after themselves. They research extensively about how to dispose of their victims and take their time to conceal the bodies. They will sometimes change their modus operandi (also known as m.o.), or their method of killing, as they learn from past mistakes and become more effective. They choose victims who will not draw as much public attention.

Serial killers also avoid capture because they typically appear normal to those around them. Rather than acting like the wild-eyed maniacs that people expect killers to be, most are ordinary. Many hold jobs and have families and friends. As Gary Van Dusen said of his neighbor, Dennis Rader, "[His arrest was] the biggest shock I'd ever had—[he was] the nicest guy in the world. I'd have given him a key to watch my dog if I had to when I was leaving town."[2] If, by chance, such killers come to the notice of the police and are taken in for questioning, they are often cooperative and are able to pass polygraph tests, also known as lie detector tests, primarily because they feel no guilt for the crimes they have committed.

Tracking serial killers who have the advantage of time and anonymity is an enormous challenge for law enforcement officers. Unlike other violent crimes, in most serial killings there is no relationship between the victim and the offender. A routine police investigation would normally start with questioning the victim's friends and family. In a serial

Serial killer Rodney Alcala, shown here, seemed so normal that he appeared on a game show called The Dating Game *in 1978. He won, but the woman chose not to go out with him because he seemed "creepy." He was sentenced to death in 2010 for the murder of five women.*

killing, the investigation has to start with the offender and the choices he or she made while committing the murder so the cases can be linked together.

There are external pressures that investigators face as well. Serial killings draw public attention, and there is enormous pressure and scrutiny from the media and higher-level law enforcement. A long serial murder investigation can also cause fear and panic in a community. For example, most victims of David Berkowitz were brunettes, so many brown-haired women around New York City put on blonde wigs before going out at night.

Investigators of serial killings need to have the same persistence, patience, and organizational skills as the killers they are trying to capture. The popularity of TV shows and movies such as *Dexter* and *Silence of the Lambs* is proof that society is fascinated by serial killers and what motivates them. Catching them, however, is nothing like a Hollywood script.

Chapter One
Serial Killer Task Force

In 2014, the Federal Bureau of Investigation's (FBI) National Center for the Analysis of Violent Crime published a study called *Serial Murder: Pathways for Investigation.* The authors of this study spent years collecting and analyzing information from hundreds of serial murder cases so that law enforcement officers could better understand the crimes and be able to solve them quicker. The study focused on one main aspect of serial killings: how and where the bodies were discovered. Robert J. Morton, retired FBI agent and co-author of the study, said,

> In the past ... research tended to focus on known offenders and what led them to become serial murderers ... What we tried to do was give investigators working these cases a common place to start, which is the body ... The body is the only constant in the crime ... Lots of other things can change, but how you find that victim is not going to change.[3]

Morton's research revealed that where and how that body is left says a great deal about the killer.

Typically, the first step in investigating a serial murder is to form a task force. Task forces are designed to focus on a particular criminal activity. Members of task forces can be from multiple agencies across extended geographical areas, depending on the scale and scope of the crimes. Each member of the task force generally has expertise in a particular area. This combination of resources and intelligence has proven to be the most effective way to catch a serial killer.

Robert D. Keppel is a retired detective who was part of the investigations of serial killers Ted Bundy and Gary Ridgway, who is known

Members of the Green River serial killer task force are shown here speaking to the media the day after Gary Ridgway pled guilty to the Green River murders.

as the Green River Killer. He said that a serial murder investigation depends on three factors: recognition, acknowledgement, and control. Keppel writes that the success of the investigation depends on the police knowing what they are dealing with, accepting the truth, and managing it once they have identified it.

By the Numbers

15

number of active serial killers in the U.S. in 2015

Assembling a Dream Team

Crime profiler John Philpin wrote, "The purpose of a homicide task force is to facilitate the work of investigators. At best, the task force centralizes information and provides the clerical and computer Support officers need. At worst, the task force becomes a venue [setting] for performing personalities."[4]

In the case of a serial murder, law enforcement agencies must work together. The FBI's National Center for the Analysis of Violent Crime (NCAVC) says that an effective task force requires the designation of a lead agency with a lead investigator and coinvestigator. Deciding on the lead agency depends on many factors, including the number of cases, resources, and overall experience of the agency's investigators. The lead investigators are responsible for all crime scene activities. They also review any incoming information, organize it, and assign leads to other investigators.

Most task forces need a computer system to track leads and tips in the case. Depending on the size of the case, additional personnel may be useful for data entry and analysis. Making sure there is enough manpower to handle the case is essential to the investigation. It might seem as if a large, widespread case requires a large number of investigators, but sometimes a smaller, more experienced group is more effective.

The NCAVC recommends assigning personnel to the people who were closest to the victims. The families are the highest priorities, and it is the job of the liaison to make them feel confident in the investigation and that everything is being done to find the killer. This person must have great interpersonal and communication skills and must maintain regular contact with the victim's

Why Do They Kill?

People are fascinated by serial killers and how their minds work. There is typically no one reason why certain people become serial killers, although many of them have similarities. About 70 percent of serial killers have suffered either physical or sexual abuse or both, and about 50 percent were psychologically abused or neglected during their childhood.

Forensic psychiatrist Dr. Helen Morrison studied and interviewed 135 serial killers, and she believes that a chromosomal abnormality is the explanation for their homicidal tendencies. This abnormality generally begins during puberty and is more evident in men who have already displayed violent behavior. Brain scans of people with this chromosomal abnormality show evidence that they are detached from the world and are not able to feel a sense of empathy, making it easier for them to kill.

Jim Fallon is a neuroscientist who has studied the brains of psychopaths for 20 years, and he found that most had low orbital cortex activity. This is the part of the brain that is involved with impulse control, ethical behavior, and decision-making. Low activity also means more difficulty in controlling violence, rage, eating, and drinking.

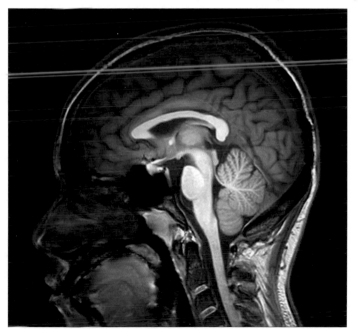

Fallon said, "People with low orbital cortex activity are either free-wheeling types or sociopaths."[1]

1. Quoted in Lizette Borreli, "Inside the Criminal Mind: Brain Scans of Serial Killers Show Low Orbital Cortex Activity, High Psychopathic Tendencies," Medical Daily, February 24, 2016. www.medicaldaily.com/serial-killer-criminal-mind-brain-scans-374994.

Studies of human brains have been used to give scientists, law enforcement officials, and the public a better sense of what the mind of a serial killer is like.

loved ones, making sure they have the most current information.

Someone also must be responsible for communication with the external supports that are vital to a serial murder investigation, including the forensics lab, medical examiner's office, and local prosecutor.

From December 20 to December 30, 2012, in Anaheim, California, 3 homeless men were slain, marking the first serial murders in Orange County, California, in the last 25 years. The task force that was assembled was comprised of officers from the Anaheim Police Department, police departments in surrounding towns, the Orange County Sheriff's Department, the FBI, and data entry and office personnel. Following the murders, the lead investigator, Detective Daron Wyatt told the force that he was instituting a "roadblock canvass." Stopping cars and interviewing people is long and tedious, but the investigators joined together and spoke with hundreds of people, which produced some new leads. When Wyatt was asked what his first step was when investigating a homicide, he said, "The first thing I do is pray that the victim's family has peace and that I find the perpetrator."[5]

By the Numbers

49

counts of murder Gary Ridgway pled guilty to

Start at the Scene

The lead investigator is responsible for making sure the analysis of the crime scene is competent and thorough. In a serial case, the focus is on the nature of the physical or sexual interaction, the choice of weapon, the way the victim was killed, and the method of body disposal. These factors are important in figuring out how much skill and experience the criminal has.

Investigators are careful not to disturb any evidence, so they generally tread a narrow path from their vehicles, making sure that nothing important is lying underfoot. If there are indications that more than one body may be on site—the discovery of two skulls, for instance—crime-scene tape is quickly strung around a wide perimeter to preserve the area. Within the perimeter, tape is also strung around each decomposition site, or set of remains.

Following those steps, each

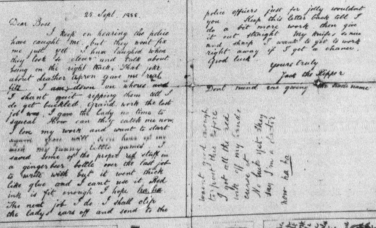

This poster was hung up during Jack the Ripper's "autumn of terror" in 1888. Task forces today still ask for help from the public in many serial killer investigations.

decomposition site is carefully examined. Sometimes the process can take days. Photos and videos are taken throughout. A medical examiner, who is responsible for determining manner of death and identity of the victim, examines the remains. These are then collected for a later autopsy in the lab. Detectives comb through the site on hands and knees, using magnifying glasses and tweezers to collect trace evidence such as hair, fingernails, and bits of bone. A metal detector is sometimes used to ensure that objects such as jewelry are not overlooked. Every article that seems significant is photographed, numbered, and carefully placed in a bag to prevent contamination. Investigators then transport it to the crime lab for analysis.

The most important factor in identifying a serial murderer is case linkage. Case linkage is the process of determining whether there are connections between two or more previously unrelated cases through crime scene analysis. Case linkage is based on factors, including the m.o., similarity of physical interactions, geographical location, and time of day.

Some serial murderers have distinct signatures, which are a sort of personal mark of the offender. Signatures are reflective of the killer's personality and are not necessary to commit the crime. Some signatures are the result of psychological deviance, others are fantasy-driven rituals, and others are purely for shock value. Although a serial killer's m.o. may change over time as they become more skilled, the signature typically remains the same. Some offenders "pose" the victim to fulfill the vision in the killer's head or to send a message to the police and public. Jack the Ripper sometimes posed his victims in a certain way to horrify onlookers and the police.

In Texas from 1990 to 1991, three sex workers were murdered. Each had their eyeballs carefully cut out of their head with almost surgical precision. Investigators knew their offender was someone who had done this many times before. A lead from another sex worker led police to Charles Albright, a former high school science teacher with a background in taxidermy and an apparent obsession with eyes.

Data Management

Some cases are overloaded with information, and a common problem in serial investigations is collecting and organizing this information in an efficient manner. Substandard data management can result in the loss of useful leads. Computer systems are the best way to organize and analyze large amounts of data. The FBI uses

Linkage Blindness

Linkage blindness, a phrase coined by Dr. Steven Egger, a criminal justice expert, is an inability or unwillingness to see facts that link crimes together, typically as a result of detectives who make little attempt to investigate crimes outside of their jurisdiction:

Linkage blindness exemplifies the major weakness of our structural defenses against crime and our ability to control it. Simply stated, the exchange of investigative information among police departments in this country is, at best, very poor. Linkage blindness is the nearly total lack of sharing or coordinating of investigative information and the lack of adequate networking by law enforcement agencies. This lack of sharing or networking is prevalent today with law enforcement officers and their agencies. Thus linkages are rarely established among different geographic areas of the country experiencing similar crime patterns or modus operandi. Such a condition directly inhibits an early warning or detection system of the serial murderer preying on multiple victims. [Today there is a national databank designed to help in the identification and investigation of serial murder. But many police departments don't bother contributing information to the computerized repository. Moreover, within federal law enforcement, there is still little coordination and cooperation between agencies.][1]

1. Steven A. Egger, *The Killers Among Us: An Examination of Serial Murder And Its Investigation*. Upper Saddle River, NJ: Prentice Hall, 2002, e-book.

a program called Rapid Start, which provides hardware and software for collecting, storing, and analyzing data. All reports on leads are entered in the Rapid Start database and are updated after the lead is verified. The program also allows the task force access to more than 1,200 public databases and information from other FBI and police offices. Resources from across the country can be used to follow leads.

In October 2002, a series of shootings took place over a three-week period in Maryland, Virginia, and Washington, D.C. Neighborhoods were terrorized as the killers, who became known as the "DC Snipers" appeared to be shooting random victims at gas stations, department store parking lots, and other public places. People were calling the police with tips and leads until the number of calls reached tens of thousands. Rapid Start enabled the task force to take all the leads, no matter how credible, and log them into the system. The information was then loaded onto FBI computers and reviewed by federal agents to determine whether they were high or low priority. Using this system, 70,000 calls and leads were reduced to 16,000 credible leads.

During an investigation, even rough, handwritten notes are still relevant and should be saved and documented. Task forces often keep murder books that have every piece of investigative information recorded. Record keeping can become a full-time job because of the enormous amounts of evidence and information that is collected in the course of a case. Gary Ridgway, or the Green River Killer, strangled more than 71 women in the 1980s and 1990s—more than any other known serial killer in history. He eventually pled guilty to 49 counts of murder. Crime writer Ann Rule described the Green River files seven years into the investigation:

> Try to imagine your own life, as if you had pressed every corsage, saved every letter, taken photos of each piece of jewelry you ever owned, every garment, dirt samples from the yard of every residence ... all the artifacts of your days on earth ... Each victim's section was *at least two thousand pages long; some were ten times that count.*[6]

Victimology

Another responsibility of a task force in a serial murder investigation is the development of a thorough understanding of the victim, or victimology. Knowing who the victim was, where they worked, and about their social relationships gives investigators insight into why they might have been victimized. Certain factors in the victim's life indicate whether they were at a low or high risk of being the victim of a violent crime. These factors include age, occupation, marital status, former relationships, prior arrest history, or history of drug or alcohol abuse.

Victimology data can provide information on how the killer chooses their victims. The FBI states that offenders choose their victims based on three main points. First is availability, or how accessible the victim is to the offender. Second is the vulnerability of the victim. Are there circumstances in that person's life making them more likely to be victimized? For example, an accountant generally has daytime business hours, but a cocktail waitress is more likely to be out alone at night, which increases her vulnerability. The third point is desirable. In certain murders, the killer may evaluate the physical attractiveness of potential victims. Other offenders may choose victims based on an underlying desire they need to fulfill.

Ex-policeman Mikhail Popkov would put on his uniform, get into his patrol car and lurk at night outside bars, concerts, or parties. He was looking for women that resembled his mother: full-figured, short in stature, and intoxicated. He would ask these women if they needed a ride home, gaining their trust as an officer, but they never made it to their destination. Police believe he was seeking revenge for the actions of his mother, who was an alcoholic and allegedly abused him. Alexander Grishin, a psychiatrist in Angarsk, Russia, said, "Maybe in his childhood other drunk women abused him too, and all this affected his behaviour later in his adult life and led to such horrible consequences."[7]

Analysis of the crime scene combined with victimology helps investigators determine if offenders are targeting specific types of victims, or if the killing was more of a crime of opportunity within a certain area. These are called hunting areas by investigators, which are areas that the killer is familiar with and uses to attack their potential victims.

Puzzle Pieces

There are many pieces to figuring out the puzzle of a serial murder, and there are key factors the task force must focus on to solve it. They must take note of the geographic location and its characteristics. Is it a city or a rural environment? Is it a racially mixed area? Can the offender get around without being noticed? They also need to figure out if a specific type of victim is being targeted or if the act is being carried out in a hunting area.

The way the offender accesses the victims offers investigators information about their abilities and behaviors. Some offenders break into homes, while others may solicit sex workers. The weapon used by the offender is another clue into the killer's mind, not just by the manner of death, but also by how the weapon was used and if the person had experience using it. These factors give insight to characteristics of an offender's background.

The way the offender interacts with a victim can sometimes indicate whether the person has had prior experience with violent crime. Finally, the way the body is disposed can reveal how familiar the offender is with the area and in other cases, reveals something about the relationship between the offender and

The NCAVC's Behavioral Analysis unit studied how the bodies of serial killer victims were disposed of after the murders as a way of learning more about the killers. For instance, it was discovered that white males between the ages of 24 and 43 are more likely to move the body away from the murder scene and hide it another location.

Ted Bundy, shown here, searched for thin, pretty women with long hair parted in the middle, but when asked about selecting victims because of their appearance, he answered that selection was a matter of opportunity.

the victim.

Because in most serial crimes there is no personal relationship between the victim and the offender, following up on missing person reports in the area can yield useful information. Former police detective Michael Nault, who was part of two serial murder investigations in Washington State, said, "There is no more important nexus [link] to find serial killers than missing persons ... The major things done wrong in the Ted Bundy and Green River cases were failures to track and identify missing persons."[8]

The Art of the Interview

Interviewing witnesses requires a balance of professionalism and compassion. Sex workers, drug users, and other people who might be involved

Many law enforcement officials worked together to find and arrest Lee Boyd Malvo, shown here, who was one of the infamous DC Snipers.

in illegal activities may be reluctant to share information for fear of being penalized. In the case of Robert Lee Yates Jr., who was convicted of murdering 16 women in Washington State, several sex workers told police about being approached by a sinister man who later proved to be the killer.

Interviewing suspects and persons of interest is even more of challenge. Investigators often begin an interview by complimenting the suspect and asking for their help. They then determine if the suspect is likely to respond to friendliness, flattery, or firmness, and they try to use the appropriate approach. If the wrong technique is used and a suspect becomes belligerent, investigators are not likely to acquire useful information.

Gary Ridgway, who eventually was identified as the Green River Killer, was a suspect as early as 1983, when rumors began to spread about a serial killer who targeted sex workers in a run-down neighborhood near Sea-Tac Airport in Seattle, Washington. Ridgway was taken in by police and interviewed after witnesses saw his truck in the area. During the interview, he admitted to soliciting sex workers, but that was it. He took and passed a polygraph test in 1984. Task force member Randy Mullinax said of Ridgway, "He had definitely compartmentalized his life. He had work. He had family. And he had killing."[9] Since Ridgway felt no remorse for his crimes, it was easy for him to pass the lie detector test.

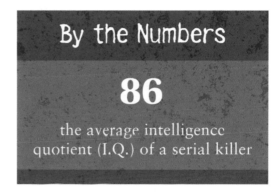

By the Numbers

86

the average intelligence quotient (I.Q.) of a serial killer

Other Resources

A task force can tap into the wisdom and skill of a host of experts, including the FBI, who have developed protocols and computer databases specific to solving serial murders. In 1985, the FBI created the Violent Criminal Apprehension Program (ViCAP) as a way of tracking and linking investigations into violent crime. In 2008, ViCAP went online and is now accessible to every level of law enforcement. When a case is added to the database, it is compared against other cases in the database, linking cases based on their m.o. or other similar traits. The results

Mistaken Identity

Former sheriff David Reichert was an investigator in the Green River killings. In his book *Chasing the Devil*, he said when the task force was briefed on their suspect, a construction worker named Bill McLean, he had his doubts. McLean did not fit the profile, and other detectives on the force felt that better suspects had been rejected. In 1986, task force members and FBI agents took McLean and his wife into custody and searched his home. After hours of questioning and interviews and five truthful polygraph tests, McLean was let go. The fact that he was almost immediately cleared did not stop the media from publishing his name and stating he was a suspect. Eventually, McLean filed a lawsuit against area newspapers, claiming they had damaged his reputation, and the public reacted against the apparent incompetence of the task force, renaming them the "Task Farce."

are forwarded to ViCAP analysts who look for patterns that could possibly link the murders. ViCAP also offers assistance in investigative support, crime mapping, and on-scene support.

Former Seattle, Washington, police officer Robert D. Keppel, is a valued consultant on many cases. Keppel was one of the lead investigators in the Ted Bundy case in Washington State in the 1970s. Bundy eluded Keppel and moved on to Utah, where he was convicted of kidnapping in 1976. He twice escaped from prison and fled to Florida, where he murdered three more young women before being caught. Bundy eventually confessed to more than 30 murders in the states of Washington, Utah, Colorado, and Florida between 1974 and 1978; he

was executed in 1989.

While working the Bundy investigation, Keppel pioneered many methods used today to track serial killers. These include the use of Explorer Search and Rescue scouts to search for evidence at a crime scene and use of the most up-to-date computer systems as organizational tools and time-savers. After leaving the police force, Keppel went on to consult on hundreds of serial murder cases, including the Atlanta Child Murders cases and the Green River Killer investigation.

Other types of consultants are more controversial. These include psychics, numerologists, astrologers, and hypnotists who may be called in when a case stalls and all other options fail. Most task force members

Trace Evidence

Locard's exchange principle was a concept formulated by 20th-century forensic scientist Dr. Edmond Locard, who was the director of the world's first crime laboratory in Lyon, France. The exchange principle means that where there is contact between two objects, there will be an exchange—fibers from clothing, hair or skin cells, fingerprints, footprints, and more. For instance, when someone sits on a sofa, a fiber or two from their clothing is likely to remain behind. When they walk across a yard, dirt particles will adhere to the soles of their shoes and then will be left on the carpet of the next house they enter. Traces of physical evidence, or "trace evidence," can tell a tale no matter how small it is. Trace evidence is a silent witness that does not lie, and it is up to the task force to find it.

Locard applied this principle himself in 1912 while he was investigating the death of a French woman, Marie Latelle. Her boyfriend, Emile Gourbin, was questioned about the murder, but he said he was playing cards with friends when it happened. Locard scraped under the boyfriend's fingernails and found skin cell samples mixed with pink blush. Locard was able to link the blush to Latelle, and Gourbin eventually confessed. Locard's exchange principal is even more critical today, as technology has made it easier to test even the most minute tissue samples.

Trace evidence is collected in several ways: Tweezers are good for catching fibers, and sometimes a piece of adhesive tape is applied to a surface, peeled off, and placed on a card for lab testing.

scorn whatever these controversial practitioners have to offer, but some authorities become desperate enough to try anything if it means catching the killer. The Boston Strangler task force called in Dutch psychic Peter Hurkos in 1963 in an effort to learn who was raping and killing women in the Boston area.

Psychic Nancy Weber was called in to help find the killer of three women in New Jersey in 1982. During the investigation she told the task force that the offender was of Eastern European heritage with a hard "k" in his name and had been arrested in New Jersey before. James J. Koedatich was eventually captured and convicted of one of the murders—the killing of a cheerleader from Parsippany Hills High School. He was of Polish descent and had been arrested for a vagrancy charge prior to the murders. Task force member Lieutenant Bill Hughes of the New Jersey Police Department described his experience with Weber on an online radio talk show: "To be honest with you, I really don't [care] what they think or what they say. I know what I saw and I know what was there. I mean, how can you be that [close-minded]? How can you be a journalist and be that [close-minded]? In this case, Nancy was on the mark on a lot of things."[10] More often than not, however, these types of consultants do little to help.

Problems Within the Force

There is little doubt that investigating a serial murder is one of the most stressful, thankless jobs in law enforcement. As long as the offender is free, there is a good chance that lives are in danger. Serial murders also tend to be high profile and there is the added pressure from the media and the public to solve the case. Task force personnel also face a tremendous amount of emotional stress. As the victims grow in number, investigators become frustrated and feel helpless or even that the murderer might never be found. These feelings can negatively impact the effectiveness of even the most experienced task force members.

Robert D. Keppel said the success of a serial murder investigation is based on recognition of the situation, acknowledgement, and management. Failure to follow any of these steps can lead to a sense of denial and defeat. In the best of circumstances, it is difficult to recognize a serial case because it may be in the middle of a killer's series. Lack of communication with other jurisdictions or an unwillingness to look for leads can prevent police from putting together what later might seem like the most obvious of clues.

Even after recognition is confirmed, Keppel said that law enforcement is sometimes hesitant to acknowledge it publicly because of the difficulties the media can bring. However, the killer continues to kill and the sense of despair heightens.

Keppel has run into bureaucratic problems as well. During an Atlanta serial murder investigation from 1979 to 1981, as many as 28 African Americans—mostly children—were killed. He has written that as the bodies continued to pile up, the Atlanta Police Department, the Georgia Bureau of Investigation, and the FBI were all in disagreement about how to catch the killer. He wrote that between the local disputes and the political forces at work in what many thought to be racially-motivated crimes, hardly any progress was made in the case. They could not even agree on the development of an initial investigative model that would allow the homicide detectives to figure out what the killer might do next.

Task force personnel often put their own lives aside to focus all their energy on catching the killer. It is not a job that they take on lightly or that does not affect them personally. David Reichert said the Green River Killer case overtook his life for 21 years and had an impact on his family. Gary Ridgway pled guilty in 2003 after DNA technology made a positive link to seven victims, ending the nightmare. However, Reichart's daughter Angela Mathena still remembers how she would have sleepless nights thinking about the killer her father was trying to catch. "I remember at one point there was a show they did on *Hard Copy* or something and Dad was on at the very end of the show," she said. "He looked right into the camera and was challenging the Green River killer and saying he was a coward and saying 'I dare you to call me, I dare you to kill me.' I remember being afraid for my life and wondering if this guy was going to come and kill my dad. But at the same time, I was thinking, 'Go Dad!'"[11]

Chapter Two
Profiling

Profiling is defined as an educated attempt to find out information on the type of person who commits certain crimes. Criminal profiling is "the practice of predicting a criminal's personality, behavioral, and demographic characteristics based on crime scene evidence."[12] According to Ronald M. Holmes, coauthor of *Profiling Violent Crimes: An Investigative Tool*, profiling has three primary uses. First, the sociological and psychological evaluation of the killer, including race, age, employment, religion, and education, will help investigators narrow the list of suspects. Second, the analysis of the objects the suspect may have had in their possession or left behind begins to tell more about what the offender may have had experience with. Third, profiling can give more insight into the offender's personality, which assists the police in how to interrogate a suspect.

Another methodology in profiling is known as the typology of the offender. This approach is based on the idea that certain types of crimes are consistent with a person's background and behavior. This type of profiling sometimes allows investigators to predict who will commit certain crimes.

In 1974, Robert Ressler developed the concept of psychological profiling while he was a supervisory agent in the FBI's Behavioral Science Unit. At that time, psychology was not as popular or as understood as it is today, especially in terms of solving crimes. Ressler and his team decided to apply psychological theory with crime scene analysis and victimology in an attempt to better understand the offender and his motives. Ted Bundy was one of the first serial killers to be profiled. Ressler interviewed him directly and said he was one the most intelligent and narcissistic criminals he had ever met. Years after the interview, Ressler said he still felt uncomfortable about the interview and was concerned that Bundy understood him better than he understood Bundy.

Robert Keppel, who took Bundy's confession, thought the profile created for Bundy fit him, "even to the point where they predicted he'd have a step-brother and that's what he had."[13]

Classifying Serial Murderers

The FBI has a system of typology that divides killers by their level of organization: organized and disorganized. Central to this theory is the idea that there are distinct differences between these two types of killers in terms of the behavioral patterns before and after the murder.

Organized killers are neat and orderly and plan their actions in advance. They have social skills that allow them to move about society and draw people in without being noticed. They bring everything they need for the killing, clean up carefully to cover any evidence, and take their weapons with them. A common method of the organized killer is to tie victims up to make sure that they do not get in the way of the fantasy. Organized killers often prolong their murders to get the most

pleasure from them. Even before a murder, they like to get to know their victims so they can savor the thought of killing them. Some move the body from the killing site and place it somewhere they have chosen ahead of time.

Jeffrey Dahmer killed 17 men and boys from 1978 to 1991 in Wisconsin. He was known to eat his victims after killing them, keeping the body parts of his victims throughout his apartment. Dahmer was an example of an organized killer. He met his victims in bars and after a few drinks, invited them up to his apartment. He would offer them a drink laced with sedatives and then would begin to torture them. Each murder was premeditated and deliberate. A personality analysis showed that he suffered from repressed hostility and severe fear of rejection and social isolation.

Chaotic crime scenes are the trademarks of disorganized killers. This is because they do not take time to plan their crimes; they strike spontaneously. This type of killer functions on impulse and rage. They have little social skills, making it difficult to lure victims. The attack is sudden, without advance planning, and the killer generally has to improvise a weapon. This weapon may or may not be left behind at the crime scene for law enforcement officials to find.

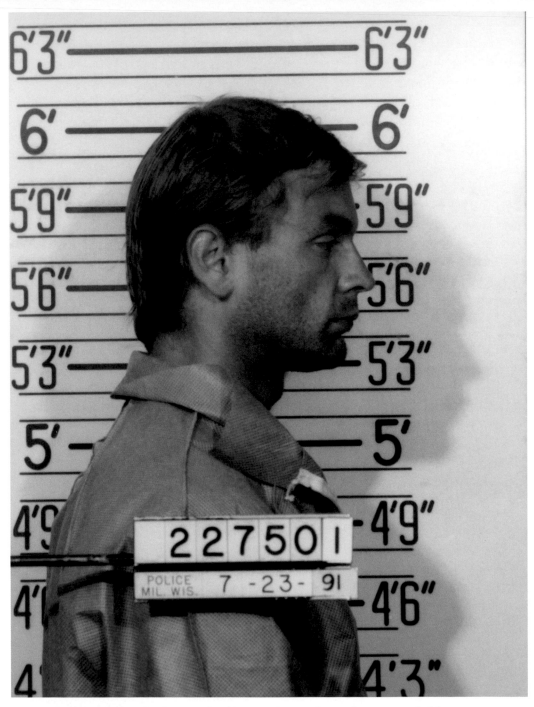

An investigation into the home of Jeffrey Dahmer, shown here, revealed human remains in the refrigerator and throughout the apartment, as well as many photos of his victims.

Organizer, Thinker, Planner

The story of Israel Keyes plays out like a movie. The *Alaska Dispatch News* reported that "a national expert on serial killers … said he was among the top three organizers, thinkers and planners he'd studied."[1] Keyes, a 34-year-old contractor from Alaska, would fly to the lower 48 states and travel by car around the country. He had stashes of "murder kits" in remote areas that he had staked out for future crimes. In between crimes, he would cut off all communication and use only cash to avoid being traced. He had no apparent motive and killed simply for the pleasure of it.

He was caught in an uncharacteristic moment of carelessness. In 2012, Keyes abducted and murdered 18-year-old Anchorage, Alaska, teen Samantha Koenig and was later caught using her debit card. He admitted to killing her, and to killing a couple in Vermont in 2011. Frank Russo, Assistant U.S. Attorney in Alaska, said Keyes also admitted to killing at least four others in Washington between 2001 and 2006 and another person in New York City in 2009. Before investigators could learn more, Keyes committed suicide in his jail cell. It was his last attempt at maintaining control. Russo said, "I feel like we lost this case … And we lost because we couldn't get these people out of his head that he kept there. That's how he described it. I have these people, they're my people, they belong to me. In killing himself, that was his answer to us: You'll never get these people out of my head."[2]

Israel Keyes kidnapped Samantha Koenig from her job at the Coffee Grounds coffee hut, shown here. He was later caught because he used her debit card.

1. Alex DeMarban, "Alaska Investigators say Keyes Felt a High from Serial Killings," *Alaska Dispatch News*, updated September 27, 2016 www.adn.com/alaska-news/article/alaska-investigators-say-keyes-felt-high-serial-killings/2012/12/08.

2. Quoted in Alex DeMarban, "Alaska Investigators say Keyes Felt a High from Serial Killings."

The scene is typically a mess. There is no attempt to clean up, and victims are left in place. There is also no clear reason for selecting victims, except for how vulnerable and accessible they are.

Herbert William Mullin killed 13 people between October 1972 and February 1973. His first victim was an elderly man who he had asked to help him with his car before beating him to death. Two weeks later, he picked up a hitchhiker, stabbed her in the heart, and again left her by the road. This behavior shows lack of planning, no real consideration in choosing his victims, and no attempt to hide his crimes. He told investigators that he needed to sacrifice these people to prevent massive earthquakes from hitting Southern California.

The Personality of a Killer

What comes to people's minds when they think of the common serial killer is someone such as Ted Bundy: young, white, male, and charming. The average person's idea of a "typical" perpetrator is a Caucasian male between the ages of 18 and 35. They may also think he was raised in a dysfunctional family and was a victim of physical or sexual abuse. Other speculations are often that he is an evil genius who makes

mistakes on purpose so the police will almost catch him or that he cannot stop murdering until he is dead or incapacitated. Most profilers agree that while serial killers share many of the same traits, there is no typical serial killer, and these myths contribute to the spread of misinformation. The Atlanta Child Killer Wayne Williams was African American. Aileen Wuornos was a sex worker who killed at least seven men who picked her up. Spokane, Washington, serial killer Robert Lee Yates came from a loving home.

Many serial killers are psychopaths, which is characterized as an antisocial personality disorder by the American Psychiatric Association (APA). Psychopaths have a disregard for the law or the rights of others, an inability to feel remorse, and a tendency towards violent behavior. They also can be narcissistic, manipulative, and emotionally shallow. Forensic psychologist Stuart Kinner noted, "Probably the pin-up boy for psychopathic people is Ted Bundy in some respects. He's clearly a very charming guy, clearly a very remorseless guy, and clearly a very manipulative guy."[14]

Few serial killers, though, suffer mental illness so severely that they are considered to be insane by the criminal justice system. To be legally insane,

Juana Barraza, a Mexican professional wrestler known as the "the Old Lady Killer," was charged in 2008 for the murders of more than 40 elderly women. When she was 12, her mother gave her away to a man, and then this man repeatedly abused her. It is believed that the murders were her way of dealing with her resentment toward her mother.

A Problem With the Typical Profile

Characteristic	All Decades	1990-2016
male	90.8%	93.5%
white	52.5%	37.4%
mid to late 20s	26.7%	24.1%
white, male	45.1%	32.8%
white, male, mid to late 20s	12.2%	7.7%

Note: Only U.S. serial killers included in this chart

According to a study by Radford University, the commonly cited profile of a serial killer in the United States being a white male in his mid to late 20s is not accurate.

Mike Aamodt, "Serial Killer Statistics," Radford University, September 4, 2016. maamodt.asp.radford.edu/Serial%20 Killer%20Information%20Center/Serial%20Killer%20Statistics.pdf.

the killer must not be aware that what they are doing is wrong while they are committing the act. Psychopaths such as Ted Bundy, Dennis Rader, or John Wayne Gacy are not insane. They kill because they have such overwhelming compulsion to kill that they ignore the consequences.

Driven to Murder

The motive of a serial murderer typically falls into one of four categories. There are killers who like to think they are ridding the world of unworthy people. They tell themselves they are doing society a favor by murdering sex workers, homosexuals, or people of a certain ethnic background. John Wayne Gacy, who killed 33 young men in Chicago between 1972 and 1978, claimed to kill for this reason. Profiler Robert Ressler interviewed Gacy after his conviction, and Gacy told him his victims were worthless. The so-called Zebra Murderers— Larry Green, J.C.X. Simon, Manuel Moore, and Jessie Lee Cooks—were part of a black extremist group in San Francisco, California, in the mid-1970s. The four maintained they were earning their way to heaven by killing as many Caucasians as possible. Their 14 victims ranged from college students to janitors. Some were shot, but others were raped and tortured.

Some serial killers are motivated by their desire for power and control. This desire stems from the fact that they feel overlooked, powerless, and unappreciated. They perceive others as constantly taking advantage of them. Their acts of violence are a form of revenge and make them feel superior. As they kill, they hold the power of life and death in their hands.

Coupled with their need for power and control, many serial killers also enjoy others' pain. The BTK Killer, for instance, chose when he wanted his victims to die. Steven B. Pennell, otherwise known as the Route 40 Killer, was an electrician who killed three women (and was linked to the disappearances of two others) in Delaware in 1987 and 1988 and also enjoyed hurting his victims. He exhibited what profilers term overkill—beating, strangling, and stabbing his victims in the course of his attacks.

Profilers recognize such emotions—and others—from the way the killer operates and the clues left at the crime scene. For instance, a perpetrator who mutilates the body after death and stages it in a humiliating position may be expressing rage. A killer who takes great risks is likely arrogant. Some serial murderers simply kill for the thrill they feel during the act. Israel Keyes got his rush by searching remote areas, sometimes hundreds of miles from his home, finding random victims, and killing them. In 2011, he drove from the West Coast to Chicago and then rented a car and drove to Vermont, where he selected a couple in their 60s and murdered them. He was suspected of at least eight murders, all committed just for fun.

Still another motivation is financial gain or better quality of life. The first widely known serial killer in the United States, H.H. Holmes, murdered his mostly female victims for their life insurance policies.

Edward Gein, shown here, was captured when he was a suspect in the disappearance of store clerk Bernice Worden in 1957. When police looked into a shed on his property, they found Worden's body.

Some serial killers do commit murder as a result of mental illness. Some, such as Herbert Mullin and David Berkowitz, claim to hear the voice of God, Satan, or a dead family member who demands that they kill for some reason.

The acts of mentally ill killers often appear bizarre and irrational to outsiders, but they make sense in the context of their disordered thinking. Wisconsin native Edward Gein was a devoted son to his mother, and after her death in 1945, his behavior became deranged. He murdered and tortured at least two women—and probably more—between 1954 and 1957. He also robbed graves and used the body parts to decorate his house. He was found legally insane and was committed to a psychiatric hospital for criminals. Ten years later, that was overturned, and he was convicted of murder and

By the Numbers

25

serial killer victims in the United States in 2016

spent the rest of his life in criminal psychiatric facilities.

Studying the Victims

Profilers study victimology in a case because it gives additional insight into the movements, motives, intent, and fantasies that drive the perpetrator to kill. If profilers understand why certain victims were chosen, they can better predict the risks a killer is comfortable taking, their sexual preferences, and their attitude toward the group the victims represent.

Victims sometimes fit stereotypes that have symbolic meaning for the killer. They may represent a class of women who the killer believes has rejected and humiliated him all his life. They may be homosexual men who are repressing themselves, as in the case of John Wayne Gacy. They may represent abusive mother figures. When studying victims, profilers first note characteristics such as appearance, occupation, personal lifestyle, and last-known activities. These facts give clues to the killer's fantasies and motives for killing.

If possible, profilers also map victims' movements just before they were murdered to find out where they crossed paths with the killer. For example, Jeffrey Dahmer met many of his victims in gay bars he frequented in Milwaukee, Wisconsin.

Careers in Criminal Profiling

Job Description:
Criminal profilers rely on psychology and experience in criminology to create a portrait of an unknown perpetrator. They perform crime scene analyses, read police reports, and research earlier cases for patterns of criminal behavior.

Education:
A bachelor's degree in behavioral science, criminology, sociology, psychology, criminal justice, or a related field, and a graduate degree in forensic psychology from an accredited college or university can help one acquire a career in profiling. Degrees with a concentration in forensic investigation, criminal procedures, and criminal law are recommended. The FBI's Behavioral Science Unit also provides training for profilers.

Personal Qualifications:
Strong analytical skills and intuition, ability to remain emotionally detached, highly developed observational skills, and an understanding of criminal minds and psychology are ideal attributes for profilers.

Salary:
The average annual salary for a criminal profiler in the United States is $80,540.

Profilers also review forensics reports, including autopsy reports, toxicology reports, photos of the autopsy and the wounds, and the findings of the coroner regarding the time and cause of death, kind of weapon, and how it was used.

Crime Scene Profiling

Investigators believe that the crime scene reflects the killer's mental pathology, so profiling based on physical evidence found at the scene is valuable. Profilers look for signs that tell them if there is a link between two or more murders. Did the killer leave a signature or did they take some "memorabilia" with them? Robert D. Keppel and William J. Birnes noted, "Signatures [are] a clue not only to what the murderer does, but what he wants, what he seeks, and what drives him from victim to victim ... Signatures are the only ways the killer truly expresses himself ... If you're smart, you can figure out what the killer is really after."[15]

Aerial photos and photos of the crime scene are vital, as well as consideration of other environmental factors including climate, topography, and weather conditions at the time of the murder.

A Mental Map

Geographic profiling is the process of analyzing locations connected in a series of crimes to figure out the most likely area in which the offender lives. The concept of geographic profiling is based on the fact that everyone has a mental map of their surroundings that develops as a result of personal experiences, travel routes, reference points, and centers of activity. People are most comfortable within the boundary of their mental map, and serial killers are most likely to hunt, attack, and dump victims within those boundaries as well.

Geographic profiling, which provides data for case linkage and psychological profiling, involves studying the murder locations, the criminal's hunting behavior, and victim selection. Profilers review maps and visit the neighborhoods around the murder scenes. They note specific details, including whether or not the weapon was found in a secluded area or whether or not a victim's body was deposited in an area with other trash. They also note barriers, such as bodies of water, high walls, or steep hillsides, that might have caused the killer to avoid one route and take another.

In 1997, Dr. Kim Rossmo, a detective from the Vancouver Police Department, developed the first geographical profiling technology for tracking serial killers. Rigel is a crime analysis program that estimates the area where the offender lives based on data about the location of the crimes. The geographic targeting system produces "jeopardy" surfaces, which are three-dimensional surfaces that highlight the most probable areas where the offender lives. Different colors on the map indicate the statistical probabilities assigned to each area, and the jeopardy surface is in red.

"The Wicked Quarter-Mile"

Geographic profiling proved its value when it guided investigators to the neighborhood of serial killer Robert Lee Yates in Spokane, Washington, in 1999. The task force was motivated to do a geographic profile because of the logos on the grocery bags on the victims' heads. They speculated that the killer had used bags that had come from stores in his neighborhood. The bags were printed with logos from Albertsons and Safeway, which were plentiful in the Spokane area. One bag was from a Super 1 Foods store, however, and there was only one outlet in Spokane County. That store was located in Spokane's residential South Hill. An investigation proved that an Albertsons and a Safeway lay within 1 mile (1.6 km) of that store as well.

After plotting the locations where the killer dumped his victims as well as the locations of the stores and other key data, the task force came up with general coordinates within which the killer was likely to live. After they had arrested Yates, they were gratified to realize how accurate their profile had been. Former Spokane police chief Cal Walker stated, "Geographic profiling led investigators to within thirteen blocks of Yates' home four months before he was even a suspect. [It helped] us prioritize persons of interest by giving special attention to those living on the South Hill."[16]

Dr. Kim Rossmo is the Director of the Center for Geospatial Intelligence and Investigation at Texas State University. One of their projects was a geographical profile of Jack the Ripper, the infamous killer who murdered and mutilated at least five sex workers in London's East End between August 7 and September 10, 1888. He was never found. A geographical profile shows the murders were within a hunting area of 0.5 square mile (1.3 sq km). The peak area was concentrated in a neighborhood full of slums, transients, and brothels known as "the wicked quarter-mile." The victims lived within 200 yards (182 m) of each other in boarding houses within the quarter mile. If geographic profiling were available in the 1800s, investigators may have been able to pinpoint the Ripper's residence to within a three-block area.

Even Rossmo knows that geographic profiling alone does not solve cases, but as a tool, it helps manage the large amount of geographical information and decodes crime patterns. Generally, profiling is never a substitute for a thorough investigation, and a profile alone is not enough to add or remove someone from a suspect list.

Robert Ressler's work as a profiler was used by John Wayne Gacy to taunt him. Ressler was given a self-portrait of Gacy as a clown with a note written on the back (Gacy dressed as a clown to lure some of his victims): "Dear Bob Ressler, you cannot hope to enjoy the harvest without first laboring in the

Visitors to the Jack the Ripper Museum in Britain are shown here looking at a map detailing the locations of the murders.

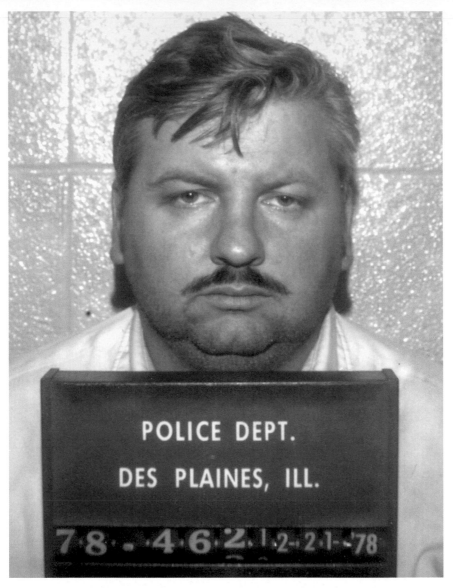

Gacy, shown here, was a successful contractor and respected friend and neighbor who threw theme parties at his home where he would dress as Pogo the Clown. This was also his way of luring victims. Eventually, 33 young men and boys were found in the crawl space under his home.

fields. Best wishes and good luck. Sincerely, John Wayne Gacy, June 1988." When Ressler asked what he meant, Gacy replied, "Well Mr. Ressler, you're the criminal profiler. You're the FBI. You figure it out."[17]

Chapter Three
Public Attention

Serial murder cases make head-lines. These cases can attract attention because of the victims or because the details of the murder may have been particularly grue-some. Sometimes the serial killers themselves attract the attention. Twenty-four hour news programs and countless Internet websites demand that the reporting industry provide more and more content. The constant public attention to a serial murder case often results in conflicts with law enforcement.

There is a long history of distrust between the law and the media. Law enforcement agencies think that the media publishes unverified and sometimes inaccurate information that could disrupt their investigation. Media organizations often feel that the police are withholding infor-mation from them and accuse them of a lack of communication. The happiest person in this relationship is the killer, because the more con-flict there is between the police and the public, the more likely they are going to be able to continue to kill. The best chance for a successful serial murder investigation is for there to be cooperation and respect between law enforcement and the media.

Media Influence and Participation

Because the media is a visible and influential part of the community, it can be an enormous help to task force members. Serial killers some-times communicate with media out-lets rather than directly with the police. Between 1969 and 1974, the so-called Zodiac Killer sent more than 20 letters to local San Francisco Bay Area publications, such as the *San Francisco Chronicle* and the *Vallejo Times-Herald* news-papers. He had murdered at least

Fascination with Serial Killers

Why do people have such a fascination with serial killers? Serial killers have had a place in popular culture for decades. The story of Edward Gein inspired characters in at least three movies, including Norman Bates in *Psycho*, Leatherface in *The Texas Chainsaw Massacre*, and Buffalo Bill in *Silence of the Lambs*. Dr. Scott Bonn, the author of *Why We Love Serial Killers: The Curious Appeal of the World's Most Savage Murderers*, said that serial killers are to adults as scary movies are to kids, and adults get a sort of guilty pleasure from following their stories. He wrote that serial killers appeal to a basic survival instinct in people. The killer's total disregard for the life and suffering of the victims causes people to question their sense of humanity and makes them doubt their safety and security.

What really fascinates people about serial killers is not just the horrific nature of their crimes, but also their humanness. Serial murderers have families, have jobs, and are members of local churches. Albert Fish, the "Brooklyn Vampire," killed children, but his neighbors thought he was a nice old man. Helen Morrison, a forensic psychiatrist, wrote about this in her book *My Life Among the Serial Killers*. Bonn added, "Look at a guy like Ted Bundy. He was very good-looking, he was successful, women were very attracted to him, which was why he was able to get 36 of them into his car [before abducting and killing them]. He looked like the boy next door, and that is frightening because if the boy next door is a serial killer, it means anyone is potentially a victim."[1]

1. Quoted in Michael Bond, "Why Are We Eternally Fascinated by Serial Killers?" BBC, March 31, 2016. www.bbc.com/future/story/20160331-why-are-we-eternally-fascinated-by-serial-killers.

five people in this region beginning in 1966. In addition to clues, the letters held fingerprints and gave details of the murders that investigators did not know. Despite that information, however, the killer was never identified.

In New York City on May 30, 1977, journalist Jimmy Breslin received a letter from Son of Sam, who was terrorizing the city at the time. The letter revealed the killer's future plans and held partial fingerprints on its surface. Breslin turned it over to police, and it helped convict David Berkowitz, who was arrested on August 10, 1977, in connection with the six killings.

Because media influence is so important in a serial murder case, the NCAVC recommends implementing a media plan, including assigning a liaison to speak to the media on behalf of the investigation. The liaison should design press releases that outline case development,

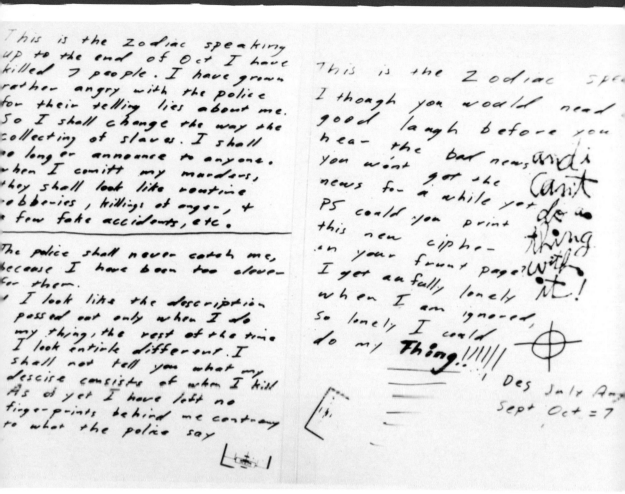

The Zodiac Killer started sending letters to police soon after his first murder, signing them with a plus sign over a circle. He also sent messages in code, taunting investigators about their inability to read them. One of his letters is shown here.

share public safety information and education, and appeal to the public to help them find a serial killer.

The BTK case is an example of how having an effective media plan helped catch a murderer. This killer actively killed between 1974 and 1991 and sent several communications to the media and police until he abruptly stopped. He came back in 2004 by contacting the media. The lieutenant in charge of the investigation worked with the media to contact the killer back and forth at critical times through press releases. The killer responded 11 times, the last time sending a computer disk that ultimately identified Dennis Rader when the disk was traced back to a computer at his church. During questioning, Rader said that he was impressed with the press releases and felt he had a positive relationship with the lieutenant.

When problems do threaten the law enforcement-media relationship, it is important to address them quickly. If the media is spreading inaccurate information, it should be acknowledged and corrected as soon as possible. In the same way, if information from law enforcement needs to be retracted, the liaison should establish communication with the media as quickly as possible. The liaison to the families of the victims should counter any media attempts to contact and interview them. Alternate methods can also be used to get information to the public, such as a regularly updated website.

Convincing the press to withhold information can be difficult. Often an agreement can be reached only if the argument is made that publishing all the details of the crime will alert the killer to the fact that the task force is closing in. Such was the case during the Robert Lee Yates investigation when former KXLY-TV reporter Cyndy Koures in Spokane,

Washington, discovered that the task force had found the serial killer's DNA on the victims, although they had not yet matched the genetic material to a name. Investigators pointed out that, if the fact was published, the killer could change his method of operating, move to another region, or go into hiding until the excitement died down. Koures agreed not to mention the DNA: "I didn't feel that the public would have benefited from that information. I asked myself, 'Is it worth this one line in this story to possibly damage or jeopardize their investigation?'"[18]

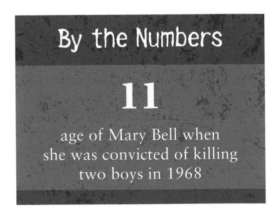

By the Numbers

11

age of Mary Bell when she was convicted of killing two boys in 1968

Problems with the Media

Mismanagement of the media during cases has several negative consequences. Providing too much information can alert the killer and cause them to change their m.o. Not providing enough information leads to a sense of frustration among the media, who may decide to try and get the facts themselves. This can seriously compromise the case, as the reporters go out on the streets or visit victims' families looking for witnesses, conducting interviews, and following leads. Sometimes reporters talk to people even before the police can interview them. In doing so, they discover and broadcast facts that the task force may want concealed. Reporters also wonder and theorize about what they hear and then ask interviewees to comment on the possibilities. Rumors spread as a result, with some of the guesswork taken as fact.

This problem has increased dramatically with the advancement of technology. There are millions of websites with writers anxious to report on any part of a serial murder case—sometimes before it has been verified. Rumors and speculation

Some believe that the heightened media coverage serial murderers receive inspires the killers to keep committing their crimes. They want to keep their names in the paper and prove that they are worthy of the "celebrity" status they have been given.

about cases can be spread around the world with just a few clicks.

The media liason on the task force has the responsibility of minimizing leaks and preventing guesswork. According to the NCAVC, every press release they make should have a specific objective and be presented in a positive tone. Liaisons should address the impact of the case on the community and public safety. They have to be able to stand up under intense questioning, even when there is little news to pass on. They must be aware that any verbal comments they make might affect the strategy outlined in the written statement. Liaisons should not have access to certain sensitive facts of the case to avoid the possibility of accidentally leaking them to the press.

There were several problems caused by the media in the Westley Allan Dodd case. Dodd killed three young boys in 1989. A few days after killing Lee Iseli, he was watching the evening news and saw a composite sketch of who the police believed to be the subject. Dodd wrote in his diary that the sketch looked like him. He decided to stay in hiding for a while, and that night, he burned all the boy's clothes. When Dodd was arrested, he was asked if he kept the newspaper articles about his killings. He answered, "I kept all the newspaper articles that I found about it."[19]

An even more horrible blunder occurred when it was time for the police to notify Lee's parents that they found his remains. Portland, Oregon, Police Detectives Mike Hefley and Tom Nelson were waiting to deliver the news sensitively and in the company of a chaplain. When they arrived at the Iseli home, *The Oregonian* had already sent a reporter over to interview the boy's father about his reaction to the discovery.

Lately, there have been a lot of references made to "talking heads" in the media. A talking head is someone that the media uses to keep public interest in a story. These commentators are willing to discuss and analyze cases as experts on the topic of serial killers and sometimes even on the case at hand, whether they have credible information or not. Some may be experts in their fields as researchers, retired law enforcement officers, and mental health professionals, but others are considered "pseudo-experts," or self-proclaimed experts in profiling or criminology with no real experience.

Either way, public discussions of a serial murder case can be detrimental. Speculation on the motive and murders causes confusion and misinformation to be spread around.

This can heighten fears in the community and cause the public to lose confidence in the investigation and in law enforcement.

By the Numbers

12

percentage of convicted serial killers who killed more than 10 people between 1960 and 2006

Taking the Task Force to Task

Although an eager press irritates task force members, they prefer it to criticism that develops the longer a case continues. Occasionally, the criticism is justified. The press was justly critical when it discovered that police had talked to Jeffrey Dahmer and one of his young victims less than one hour before the victim's death. The young man, who had been drugged, was released back into Dahmer's care. The Spokane press also had the right to be critical when they learned that an error in a police report caused task force members, who were investigating owners of white Corvettes, to miss that Robert Lee Yates drove a white Corvette. These cases might have been solved years sooner and several lives could have been saved.

The feelings of distrust and dislike between the police and the media during the Green River case were mutual. The police intensely disliked the press, with one task force member even commenting that a reporter with little to do would try to capitalize on anything they could during the investigation. The Seattle newspapers and news channels were becoming impatient with the lack of progress in the case, and the police would, in turn, tell the media how and why they did not initially report the findings of the first few victims to them. News agencies complained to higher-level law enforcement that they were not being provided access to the Green River case detectives.

The Long Island Serial Killer has frustrated the police and public alike. The person responsible for 10 dead bodies found in 2010 near Long Island's Gilgo Beach is still at large. Most of his victims were female sex workers who he found on the website Craigslist, and the families of the victims have criticized the Gilgo Beach task force for incompetence and for not caring about the case because

The Seven Phases of Serial Murder

Dr. Joel Norris, a leading expert in serial sexual murder, identified seven steps a serial killer follows when committing their crime. His research was based on interviews with modern serial killers, and the steps are:

1. The Aura Phase: The potential killer begins to withdraw from reality and enters their own world of fantasy.
2. The Trolling Phase: The offender follows the victim until the time appears right for the attack. During this time, the victim is depersonalized and becomes nothing more than an object in the killer's mind.
3. The Wooing Phase: Once they have identified their victim, they try to win over their confidence and lure them into a trap.
4. The Capture Phase: The killer springs their trap.
5. The Murder: This is the moment of taking the victim's life.
6. The Totem Phase: The killer's triumph fades quickly, so to prolong the pleasure, they often take a souvenir as a trophy.
7. The Depression Phase: Post–homicidal depression overtakes the killer and triggers the cycle of phases to start again.

of what the women did for a living. Suffolk County Police Chief Stuart Cameron responded, "We absolutely do care … We want to solve these cases. We know these girls have families, and we want to bring whoever did it to justice. So that criticism is completely unjust."[20]

The Baton Rouge Multi-Agency Task Force came under criticism as it tracked Derrick Todd Lee in 2003, although members tried to be flexible in their approach. They ran informational billboard advertisements, took DNA samples from at least 1,000 individuals, released details of the case to invite tips, and investigated numerous men with suspicious backgrounds.

Former FBI profiler Gregg McCrary observed that fault finding is almost inevitable in such cases: "Whether you capture a killer after 11 homicides or after two, it's never quickly enough. Those who criticize the most typically have the least appreciation for the daunting complexity of this type of investigation."[21]

Working with the Public

Task force members are aware that, just like the press, the public can be both helpful and hurtful to a serial killer investigation. On the positive side, the public is essentially the eyes and ears of the task force, which cannot be every place all the time. Truckers on their routes are liable to notice a vehicle parked in a secluded place at night. Sex workers working the streets know who the threatening men are. Family members can say if a husband and father acts suspiciously or hides sinister activities behind his apparently ordinary exterior. FBI profiler John E. Douglas observed, "Your greatest partner in solving any crime of violence is the public. Somebody has seen something. Somebody knows something. Undoubtedly many people have seen this perpetrator and looked right through him."[22]

Unless members of the public are informed, however, they do not know who or what to look for. Police learned after arresting John Wayne Gacy that his neighbors had been repelled by a foul odor that hung around his home. They assumed the problem had to do with his drain, not decaying bodies that were buried in the crawl space under the house.

After BTK killer Dennis Rader was arrested, investigators discovered that he had been known as a "bureaucratic bully" who frightened some of his neighbors. One woman recalled that he had had her dog put to death without consulting her, simply because it escaped from her yard. Another woman remembered that she had caught him peeking in her windows and that he had stalked her because he did not like her boyfriend.

To motivate the public to share what they know or suspect, authorities hold press conferences and create public service announcements. They ask for help. They give information such as where the killer struck in the past, how many lives he or she has taken, and who is at risk in the future. They show eyewitness sketches of the killer. They publish hotline numbers where information can be called in. They even post rewards and appeal directly to the killer to turn himself in.

The Green River Killer task force used such techniques when it put together the television special "Manhunt Live: A Chance to End the Nightmare," which aired in 1988. Designed to give the struggling investigation new momentum, the program drew 50 million viewers and generated more than 1,500 leads. Other task forces have relied on television shows such as

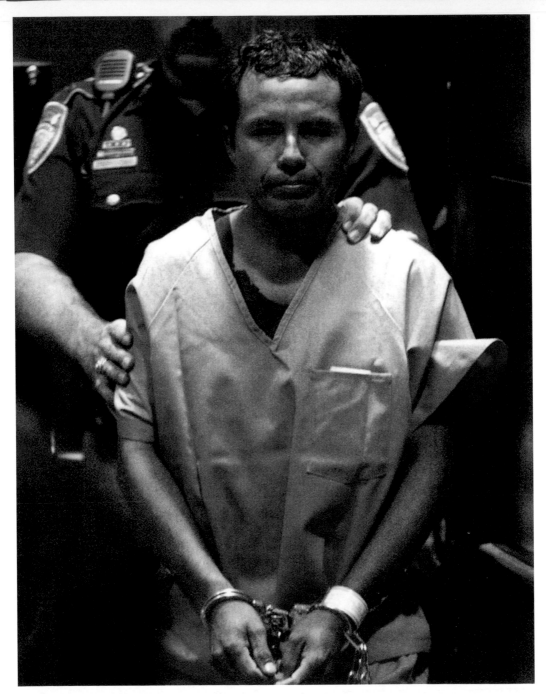

Ángel Maturino Reséndiz, the Railroad Killer, was captured soon after he was placed on the FBI's most wanted list and featured on America's Most Wanted. *He confessed to 15 murders, most occurring near railroad tracks.*

Unsolved Mysteries, which ended in 2010, and *America's Most Wanted*, which ended in 2012, to draw public attention to their cases. Canadian pig farmer and alleged sex-worker-killer Robert Pickton; the Railroad Killer, Ángel Maturino Reséndiz; and the BTK killer, Dennis Rader, were three serial killers profiled on *America's Most Wanted*. Social media has played a role in catching serial killers, as well. Mark Dizon, accused of killing nine people in the Philippines in 2010, was caught when a family friend of one of the victims saw his photo on Facebook. The photo was shown to witnesses who identified him as the man they saw running from the scene.

Over time, serial killers are sometimes caught with the help of the public. In the hunt for Richard Trenton Chase in California, a young woman responded to the published description of the suspected killer and named Chase, her former high school classmate, whom she had seen at a shopping center. In the Unabomber case, in which an unidentified serial bomber wounded 24 people and killed 3 more over the course of 17 years, the publishing of his manifesto in the *New York Times* and the *Washington Post* newspapers in 1995 led David Kaczynski to recognize the writing style of his brother Theodore.

David Kaczynski remembered, "We shared our suspicions with the FBI agents and helped them investigate and ultimately arrest my brother. Ironically, a 17-year manhunt ... was powerless to catch the Unabomber ... until an anguished family came forward, willing to turn over a loved one because it recognized its responsibility to protect others."[23]

The BTK case had been unsolved for 30 years when Wichita, Kansas, attorney Robert Beattie realized that many of the students in the political science class he was teaching were unaware that the killer was still at large. In 2003, he began writing a book about the case and was prominently featured in the local media. The next year, the publicity caused the killer to break his 13-year silence and send a letter to the *Wichita Eagle* newspaper. Further communication followed, and with new evidence to go on, authorities made an arrest in February 2005. Former Wichita police chief Floyd B. Hannon Jr., who had hunted BTK from 1974 until 1976, said to Beattie in 2005, "Without your interest in writing a book and ... also causing the person who committed the crimes to start showing off, this case might still not be solved. For this I thank you."[24]

What's In a Name?

To give punch to their stories, members of the media like to tag serial killers with catchy nicknames, such as the following:

- Boston Strangler (Albert DeSalvo): He murdered 13 women in the Boston area by strangling them, most of them with their own stockings.
- The Freeway Killers (William Bonin, Patrick Kearney, Gregory Miley, James Munro, and Randy Steven Kraft): They sexually assaulted and killed young male hitchhikers and left their bodies on the freeway.
- The Lipstick Killer (William Heirens): After the brutal murder of one of his victims, Heirens left a message for police written in lipstick: "For heaven's sake catch me before I kill more. I cannot control myself."[1]
- The Cleveland Torso Murderer: Never identified, this killer dismembered his victims.
- Son of Sam (David Berkowitz): Berkowitz claimed that his neighbor, Sam Carr, was an agent of the devil and gave him orders to kill through his Labrador retriever.

1. Quoted in Douglas Martin, "William Heirens, the 'Lipstick Killer,' Dies at 83," *New York Times*, March 7, 2012. www.nytimes.com/2012/03/07/us/william-heirens-the-lipstick-killer-dies-at-83.html.

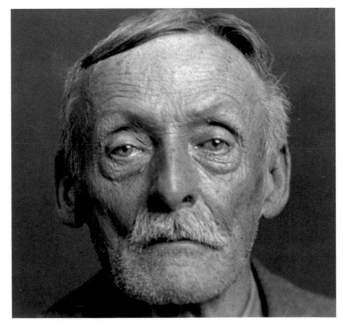

Albert Fish, shown here, was known as the Gray Man, the Werewolf of Wysteria, and the Brooklyn Vampire.

Unlikely Suggestions

However, public involvement can also cause complications. Sometimes they panic when they hear the news that a serial killer is on the loose, such as the Wichita residents who boarded their windows and purchased guns during the BTK killer case in the 1980s. Los Angeles, California, residents lived in fear when the Hillside Strangler was claiming victims in the late 1970s. Sales of burglar alarms skyrocketed. Many women took self-defense classes. Men purchased revolvers, switchblade knives, and baseball bats to arm their wives and girlfriends.

Even when the public does not panic, results of the publicity—generally thousands of tips and suggestions—can overwhelm investigators. Many of these submissions are bizarre and a waste of the task force's time. During the Green River Killer investigation, for instance, an amateur detective from Tacoma, Washington, insisted that the killer was simply a robber intent on stealing sex workers' jewelry. He urged investigators to stake out pawnshops if they wanted to catch him. In the Robert Lee Yates case in Spokane, a tipster suggested the task force place a department store mannequin on a corner and wait for the killer to attack it. Former Spokane police chief Cal Walker said, "Do you

discard this stuff? No. But you give it the weight it appears to have."[25]

Although unlikely suggestions may be ignored, some tips warrant investigation, even if the investigation has to be done internally. Mikhail Popkov avoided capture for years even when it was suspected that the killer might be someone in law enforcement. Finally, in 2012, detectives took DNA samples from 3,500 current and retired police officers, which linked Popkov to the murders.

A similar investigation took place in the BTK case, when task force members were asked to give a DNA sample to be positively ruled out as suspects. "We are collecting swabs to eliminate with certainty personnel who were employed during the time period in which the BTK murders occurred,"[26] explained Lieutenant Ken Landwehr, who headed the investigation in 2004.

BTK investigators learned by experience that even the most seemingly credible tips need a thorough follow-up. In 1978, a middle-aged woman who lived with her husband in Wichita came forward, claiming that she was being harassed and stalked by someone. One of the theories was that it was the BTK killer. She not only produced letters and poems that he had allegedly mailed

Catching the Green River Killer, shown here, took the task force almost 30 years. At one point, they had leads pointing to more than 12,000 suspects.

to her, but she also had to be rushed to the hospital after the killer apparently assaulted her and stabbed her in the back. For three years, members of the task force worked to protect her while using her leads to track the perpetrator. Finally, they became suspicious and determined that the woman had actually sent the poems to herself.

Suspicious Suspects

Involving the public in a case not only brings in thousands of tips, but it also triggers false confessions. Some of these confessions come from individuals who are mentally ill. Some are guilt-ridden or full of self-hatred. Some want attention. They distract investigators from pursuing more valuable leads.

Investigators in the Boston Strangler case were plagued with suspects who confessed to being the killer. Even today, some people question whether Albert DeSalvo, who admitted to and was convicted of the crimes, was actually one of the false confessors. In the Green River Killer case, serial killer Henry Lee Lucas, in prison in Texas, told authorities that he had committed the murders. Although Lucas was guilty of other killings, investigators who interviewed him eventually determined he had not been in the Pacific Northwest at the time of the Green River assaults. As part of the Robert Lee Yates case, investigators flew to South Dakota in response to information that a resident of that state was bragging that he had killed sex workers in Spokane. An interview and a blood sample were enough to prove the man was lying.

With today's technology, investigators rely on blood analysis rather than confessions and eyewitness testimony to determine whether they have a perpetrator correctly matched to a series of crimes. Such analysis is slow and methodical and does not rate the attention that a profiler or a police spokesperson gets. Nevertheless, it is through lab analysis that many mysteries are solved. Author and commentator Stanley Crouch wrote, "The crime lab [analysts] have the very important job of measuring and evaluating. What they bring forward can lead to putting an unmoving collar around the neck of a killer who may have gone on to live a very new life after snuffing out someone else's."[27]

Chapter Four
The Crime Lab

Arguably the most important part of a serial murder investigation is what happens in the crime laboratory. All the evidence collected at the crime scene must be analyzed. The people responsible for this process are called forensic scientists. Forensic science applies scientific analysis to the criminal justice system, generally to help solve a crime. Forensic scientists study and interpret the evidence—from blood and saliva to paint chips and tire tracks. With their scientific background, knowledge of the law, and some high tech equipment, forensic scientists can take the tiniest bit of evidence and catch the most cunning killers.

Forensic science has been around for hundreds of years. In 1892, Sir Francis Galton was the first to establish a way of classifying fingerprints. In the 1920s, chemist Philip O. Gravelle invented a comparison microscope, which consists of two microscopes joined by a common eyepiece, with the support and guidance of American doctor Calvin Goddard. This microscope could help identify which bullets came from what shell casing. In 1932, the FBI opened its first crime laboratory, and now it is one of the largest crime labs in the world, with special agents and experts traveling the globe to help support law enforcement.

What Is the Scope?

After evidence found at the crime scene is photographed, logged, and transported to the lab, analysts begin their work by focusing on the most easily lost or destroyed material. Much of this evidence is trace evidence, meaning it is small, often microscopic items such as hair, fibers, metal filings, pollen, or cosmetics. Great care is always taken while working with trace evidence, because a careless movement or a breeze from an air vent can cause something such as a chip of paint or a particle of dirt to be blown away and lost.

Analysts rely on a variety of microscopes when scrutinizing trace evidence. In addition to a traditional compound microscope, which uses light reflected and magnified through a series of lenses, they utilize comparison microscopes. Under such microscopes, two objects can be viewed at the same time, and differences and similarities can be easily noted. Analysts also use stereoscopic microscopes, which have double eyepieces and double lens systems to better scrutinize three-dimensional images. Electron microscopes, which are found in the best-equipped labs, are invaluable for examining oddly-shaped evidence. These microscopes utilize a beam of highly energized electrons to magnify objects up to 100,000 times, thus revealing their structure, composition, and surface features.

Forensic microscopist Skip Palenik relied on the infrared microscope in his lab when he was asked to analyze tiny paint specks found on victims during the Green River Killer investigation. Infrared microscopes work with the aid of photoelectric cells to measure the light absorption of evidence that may be no larger than a micron (0.00004 inch, or 0.000001 meter) in size. Palenik, who was able to match the specks with paint found on Gary Ridgway's work coveralls, concluded, "Most of the samples turned out to be made of Imron paint, a very rare type that was used extensively in the paint shop where Ridgway worked at Kenworth Trucks. Working with Dupont, who manufactured the paint, we were able to tie the samples to paint that Ridgway had been using around the time of the murders."[28]

Hairs of Evidence

Hair is examined with a comparison microscope so that it can be determined whether two people came into close contact with one another. Hair samples can also tell other things about the crime, for example, a hair that has fallen out naturally looks different from a hair that has been pulled out violently. Human hair can also tell the investigator the killer's racial characteristics.

Hair helped convict the so-called Texas Eyeball Killer, Charles Albright, in 1991. Albright earned his nickname because he was known to have an abnormal obsession with eyes. In the three murders linked to him, the victims' eyes had been surgically removed. Not only was Albright's hair found on one of his victims, but the victim's hair also was

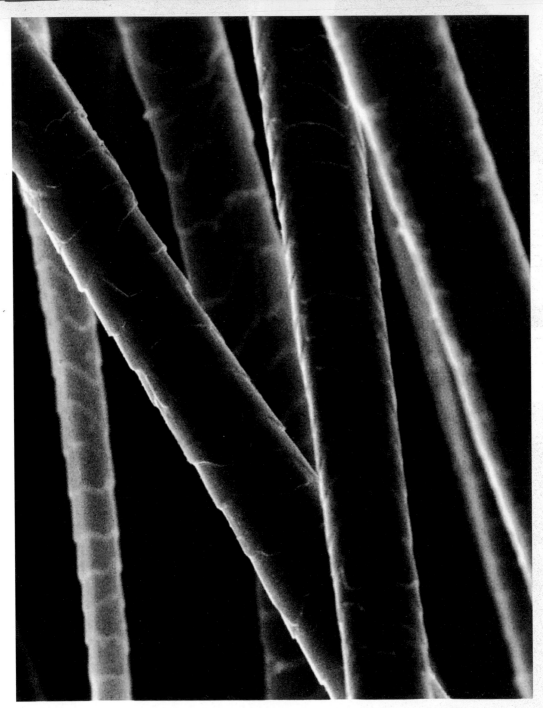

With a comparison microscope, hairs can be viewed side by side so the scientists can view the microscopic differences more clearly.

found in Albright's vacuum cleaner and on a blanket in his truck.

Analysts also microscopically scrutinize fibers found at a crime scene to link a killer to their crimes. They first concentrate on shapes. For instance, cotton or flax fibers look like blades of grass under magnification, and nylon or polyester fibers are extremely uniform and smooth. Analysts also look at color, which can be analyzed using a microspectrophotometer, which is a combination of a microscope and a spectrophotometer (an instrument that helps identify a substance by directing a beam of light at it and obtaining what is known as its absorption spectrum). Analysis of 28 different types of fibers that were eventually linked to 19 items in the home and vehicles of Atlanta Child Killer Wayne Williams helped convict him of his crimes in 1982. Bright blue fibers found on one of

several women who were killed in Delaware between 1987 and 1988 led to the arrest of Steven B. Pennell, who owned a van carpeted with such fibers.

Learning from the Landscape

Trace evidence ranges from plant debris to makeup and gunshot residue. Seen under a microscope, each piece is unique in some way and can often provide clues about the victim, the perpetrator, and the crime.

Plant material played a part in helping bring serial killer Robert Lee Yates to justice in 2000. The task force on this case noted three victims were found partially covered with yard debris, and they speculated that the material could have come from around the killer's home. Botanist Richard Old was asked to analyze the material, and from the mix, he identified leaves from Norway maple, honey locust, laceleaf maple, and Eastern white cedar trees. He also found landscaping bark with distinctive diagonal cuts, peanut shells, cherry pits, white paint chips, and pieces of concrete. Old said, "We ended up with a wonderful picture of what this yard looked like, but we didn't know what it meant."[29]

Investigators discovered the meaning in 2000 after blood from one of

By the Numbers

32

number of states that require people arrested for felonies to provide DNA samples

Sir Francis Galton, a 19th-century anthropologist, said that the chances of 2 fingerprints being identical are as small as 64 billion to 1. In more than 100 years of recorded fingerprinting, no 2 prints have ever been alike.

At a crime scene, visible fingerprints are considered a true find because in many cases, prints exist but are latent (invisible). Analysts must try to find them using a variety of chemicals and techniques. Ninhydrin is widely used for making fingerprints visible on paper surfaces. Cyanoacrylate esters, otherwise known as superglue, have proven effective for developing prints on nonporous surfaces.

Richard Ramirez, also known as the Night Stalker, committed several rapes and murders between 1984 and 1985. His last crime involved a couple who both survived and saw Ramirez's car, while another witness took down the license plate number. The car was found abandoned and, using cyanoacrylate, the police got a partial fingerprint from the interior. The Los Angeles Police Department put the print in their new automated fingerprint database, and a match was found in minutes. This case was the first to use such technology.

In the Robert Lee Yates case, analysts relied on a technique called vacuum metal deposition, which uses small amounts of gold and zinc dust, to look for latent fingerprints on the thin plastic bags covering the victims' heads. Task force member Fred Ruetsch said, "It used to be that you couldn't recover fingerprints from plastic bags, but now scientists have a new high-tech way to recover [them]."[32] On one of the bags, investigators raised a partial fingerprint and a palm print that were later matched to Yates.

Forensic Dentistry

Bite marks can also be unique enough to help convict a serial killer. A bite mark on human skin is a strong indication of guilt, because bites are not linked with ordinary daily activities.

Investigators often find bite marks in serial murder cases where a female victim has been sexually assaulted and killed. When any semicircular bruise or wound about 2 inches (5.08 cm) in diameter is discovered, they call in a forensic dentist. The forensic dentist can tell a lot about a person's teeth based on their bite mark. Crooked or chipped teeth make different impressions. The pressure of the biter also affects the impressions. A clear impression of bite marks means a lot of pressure was applied during the bite, a noticeable impression means violent pressure was used to bite.

A forensic dentist uses special lights to bring up details that are invisible under normal light. Shannon Rasp wrote, "Ultraviolet light can help law enforcement when it comes to forensic dentistry, illuminating bite marks that are invisible to the naked eye."[33]

Once positively identified, a bite mark can reveal a unique pattern of cuts and bruises that are not easily reproduced by someone else's teeth.

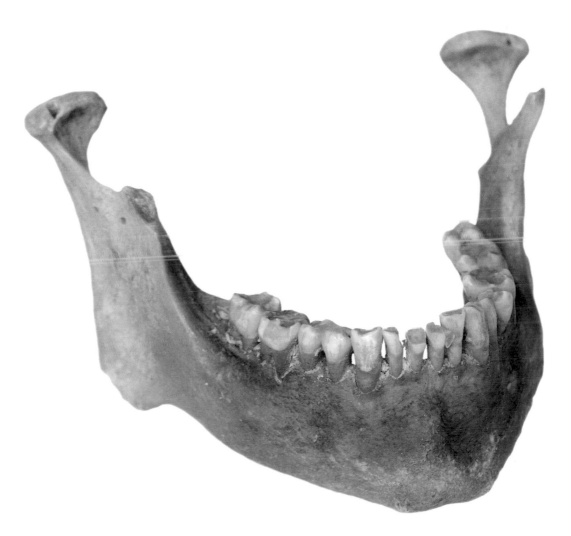

Tooth enamel is the hardest substance in the human body, which is why it is left after most of the rest of the body has decayed. Teeth can withstand very high temperatures, which is why victims of fires are often identified by their teeth.

Forensic dentist Veronique Delattre explained, "There are 28 teeth, plus four wisdom teeth, in an adult's dentition [set of teeth] ... Each tooth has five surfaces ... Each surface has its own characteristics and may have fillings, crowns, extractions, bridges, etc."[34] In addition to surface irregularities, teeth can vary in size, spacing, and alignment. A person with prominent canine teeth will leave exceptionally large, dark bruises or even lesions where those teeth press.

Forensic dentists investigate a bite by creating a mold of the suspect's upper and lower teeth, then placing that mold over a photo of the wound. If the mold fits the bite mark exactly, it is considered a match. It is important to note that bite marks are not like fingerprints or DNA and cannot provide enough information to get a 100 percent match. Critics of bite mark analysis say it should be used to rule out a suspect, rather than identify them. Roy Brown was convicted of murder in 1992 based on a bite mark left on the victim, however, he was released from prison in 2007 because DNA evidence later showed that his saliva did not match the saliva found on the bite mark. After the Brown exoneration, chief forensic dentist Richard Souviron of the Miami-Dade Medical Examiner's Office told the *New York Times*, "If

you say that this bite fits this person and nobody else in the world, and if you use the bite mark as the only piece of physical evidence linking an attacker to his victim, that's not science—that's junk."[35]

However, a bite mark left on the body of 20-year-old Lisa Levy was key evidence that helped convict Ted Bundy. Bundy bit his victims both during and after his murders. When the wounds on Levy were compared to an impression of Bundy's teeth, they were shown to be a perfect match. Author Katherine Ramsland wrote, "This was the first case in Florida's legal history that relied on bite-mark testimony, and the first time that a physical piece of evidence actually linked Bundy with one of his crimes."[36]

DNA Analysis

Biological evidence has become as important as fingerprints and bite marks when a task force is tracking a serial killer. This type of evidence includes blood, bones, semen, and mucus.

The medical examiner is the first to determine if biological evidence is present when the remains of a victim are found. After supervising the collection of the remains, he or she performs an autopsy, which is a postmortem (after-death) medical

Newest Technologies in Forensic Science

As modern technology continues to improve and enhance our daily lives, forensic technology has become so advanced that some of these innovations seem like they were created in a science-fiction movie.

Alternative light source photography uses blue light and orange filters to show bruises below the skin before they are evident to the naked eye. This allows medical professionals to see more quickly how much physical injury a victim has suffered.

The Video Spectral Comparator 2000 allows scientists to examine a piece of paper for hidden writing, the writing style based on "lift" and indentation, and the origin of the paper, even after the paper has been damaged by water or fire.

Magnetic fingerprinting dust and no-touch wanding helps investigators get higher quality fingerprints from a crime scene without contamination.

High speed ballistics photography is used by gunshot experts to match bullet trajectories and to understand how a specific bullet hole or gunshot wound was created.

examination of the corpse.

Different chemicals are used to detect different bodily fluids. Technicians use acid phosphatase to detect semen. If the test turns purple, it is positive. A chemical called phenolphthalein, whichis normally colorless, turns pink when it touches blood. Luminol is another chemical that can be sprayed around the room to detect blood, even after the killer has tried to clean up.

When biological material is found during the autopsy, the medical examiner collects it and sends it to the lab for DNA analysis. DNA, or deoxyribonucleic acid, is genetic material that is unique to each individual and can identify a killer. DNA can also be used to identify a victim because it is present in all cells, including bones and the roots of hair. No two people can have the same DNA except identical twins. Forensic scientists can identify someone from the tiniest blood or tissue samples with a technique called polymerase chain reaction (PCR). This procedure can make millions of copies of DNA from a miniscule sample of genetic material.

The ability of investigators to use DNA as an identification tool has had a revolutionary effect on bringing killers to justice. After almost 20 years, the Green River task force was

A serial killer in Germany called "the Phantom" was linked by DNA to nearly 40 murders. Police notified the public about the reward for their capture, and profilers from all over came to help solve the case. Later it was discovered that the DNA sample swabs were tainted in a factory in Austria, making the DNA evidence useless.

able to arrest Gary Ridgway when analysts matched his DNA to DNA found on the bodies of three of his victims. In 2003, DNA analysis connected Chester Dewayne Turner to 13 murders that took place in Los Angeles between 1987 and 1998. Other serial killers arrested due to DNA evidence include Dennis Rader, Robert Lee Yates, John Eric Armstrong, Lorenzo Gilyard, and Arohn Kee. Detroit police arrested Armstrong for at least five murders he committed in the 1990s. Gilyard was charged with killing 13 women in Kansas City, Missouri, between 1977 and 1993. Kee killed at least three women in New York City between 1991 and 1998.

Although most DNA analysis is carried out with nuclear DNA, there are times when mitochondrial DNA (mtDNA)—DNA found outside the nucleus of a cell—is used to identify murder victims and link killers to crimes. MtDNA is found in mitochondria (structures that provide energy in the cell) and is passed unchanged from a mother to her children. If a suspect or a victim is not available to match to DNA found at a crime scene, mtDNA from a mother or sibling can be assessed for identification purposes.

MtDNA was used to convict serial killer Hadden Clark of the murder of six-year-old Michele Dorr in Maryland in 1999. After bloodstains on the floorboards of his brother's home were found to match DNA samples from Dorr's mother, Clark confessed to stabbing the girl and later led police to her body. Clark is believed to have killed as many as a dozen women and girls on the East Coast between the mid-1970s and 1992.

Another case where mtDNA was used was to identify Gao Ghengyong, also known as the "Chinese Jack the Ripper," who raped and murdered 11 women in Baiyin City, China between 1988 and 2002. Ghengyong was finally convicted of the crimes on April 25, 2017, after being arrested in August the year before. One of his close relatives had committed a crime, and the police collected his DNA. Once they realized this relative's DNA closely matched the DNA of the killer they had been searching for, they later connected it to Ghengyong.

Forensic Anthropology

In many serial murder cases, a long period of time passes before victims are found. With nothing but bones left to analyze, forensic anthropologists are often called in to help with identification. Forensic anthropology is the study of human remains

Cold Case Solved

In 1990, three sex workers were murdered in the Spokane, Washington, area. The three women were shot to death with a .22 caliber handgun. The killings were committed around the same time and in the same area that convicted serial killer Robert Lee Yates was killing sex workers, so at the time, authorities thought the murders were connected to Yates. Biological evidence was collected and stored, even though DNA testing was uncommon at the time, but the case was never solved. In March 2012, a woman named Donna Perry was arrested on federal charges of illegal firearms. DNA evidence from that case eventually linked Perry to the murder of one of the women, Kathleen Brisbois. They also discovered that Perry had undergone gender affirming surgery in 2000 and was previously known as Douglas Perry. Investigators searched her home and found items that they believed Perry kept as trophies. The investigation also led to the discovery of a car that once belonged to Perry. After getting a search warrant, the police found .22 caliber ammunition— the same type that killed the three women—in the car. Currently, Donna Perry has not been tried and claims that Douglas Perry, the person she identified as before her surgery, had committed the crimes. When questioned by the police, she said, "I'm not going to admit I killed anybody, I didn't. Donna has killed nobody." When asked if it was Doug who killed the women, Perry replied, "I don't know if Doug did or not, it was 20 years ago and I have no idea whether he did or did not."[1]

1. Quoted in Susan Donaldson James, "Transgender Defense: 'Donna' Says 'Doug' Is the Spokane Serial Killer," ABC News, March 19, 2014. www.abcnews.go.com/Health/transgender-woman-male-persona-serial-killer/story?id=22959423.

involving skeletal analysis and techniques in archaeology to solve criminal cases. Stanley Rhine, professor emeritus in the Department of Anthropology at the University of New Mexico, explained: "In those cases in which soft tissue has been degraded by time, temperature, environment or other external forces, the only tissue remaining more or less intact is bone. The obvious person to call in to evaluate such material is the bone specialist."[37]

A forensic anthropologist can learn a great deal from a human skeleton, even if it is incomplete. They can estimate age by looking at joints. These are more worn in older people than in younger people. They can also look at the skull for indications of age and race. Sutures (where the bones join) continue to close throughout life, so a smooth skull indicates an older person. Caucasian skulls are relatively elongated; the lower jaw of African skulls juts forward in a trait called prognathism; Asian and Native American skulls are round with flat cheekbones. Sex can be determined by looking at pelvic bones, which are lower and wider in women and narrower in men. Height and body type can be estimated by measurements of the long bones in the legs.

Through such observations, forensic anthropologists can typically determine if the remains are likely one of the killer's victims. If a match is possible, DNA analysis can be carried out with good results. Although nuclear DNA is extremely difficult to come by when working with bones, there is generally enough usable mtDNA to create a profile, even if the bones are old or degraded.

Sometimes identification can be made without DNA analysis. When Jeffrey Dahmer informed police that his first murder had taken place in 1978 in his hometown of Bath, Ohio, they went in search of evidence to prove this killing. Dahmer had told them that he had killed and dismembered an 18-year-old hitchhiker named Steven Hicks and scattered his bones in a wooded area near his home. In 1991, that area was searched, and investigators found small pieces of human bones. Some were less than 0.5 inch (1.27 cm) long.

Investigators asked Douglas Owsley, an anthropologist at the Smithsonian Institution in Washington, D.C., to examine the bone fragments. In his lab, Owsley discovered some bore cut marks that supported Dahmer's statement that he had dismembered Hicks. When he pieced the fragments together, Owsley also determined that the bones were male and consistent with Hicks's height and age. Finally, he obtained medical and dental X-rays taken of Hicks before he disappeared and compared them to fragments of teeth and vertebrae that had been recovered. The match was exact, and authorities were able to announce that a positive identification of Hicks had been made.

Even with scientific advances such as DNA analysis, serial killers got away with murder for years because they killed in a variety of locales—even in different states. In the past, there was no easy way to determine if a missing person in Ohio, for instance, was linked to a murder in Chicago. Investigators had to rely on telephones, the mail, or wire services if they wanted to communicate with each other, and they seldom, if ever, shared files. Bobby Joe Long, who brutally killed 10 women in Florida in 1984, bragged, "All I had to do was throw my stuff in a car

Forensic anthropologists are able to learn a lot from skeletons such as these, even if they only have partial skeletons to examine.

By the Numbers

138

number of confirmed murders committed by the worst serial killer in history, Luis "the Beast" Garavito, between 1990 and 1999 in Colombia

and move to Lakeland or Miami or Daytona or out of state and they'd never track me down."[38]

The development of computer databases and software programs has aided communication between law enforcement agencies across the country and the world. Modern tools that forensic scientists use to solve crimes today could only be imagined 20 years ago.

Chapter Five

Forensic Technology

In 2002, the police and FBI captured suspected serial killer Maury Troy Travis in high-tech fashion. In St. Louis, Missouri, starting in April 2002, the bodies of young women began to turn up in the bushes on the sides of roadways. The police suspected a serial killer but had few leads. The following month the *St. Louis Post-Dispatch* ran a story about one of the victims, Alysia Greenwade. Within a few days, reporter Bill Smith received an envelope in the mail.

The stamp of the American flag was upside down, and the return address mentioned a website that was sexual in nature. The letter contained elaborate drawings of flowers, rakes, and a beehive with a note typed in red: "Nice sob story ... I'll tell you where many others are ... To prove I'm real here's directions to number seventeen."[39] Enclosed was a map of nearby West Alton, Illinois, marked with an "X." Police went to the spot and found a skeleton.

However, DNA did not lead the investigators to the killer in this case. Instead, they focused on the map. Investigators discovered the map was downloaded from Expedia.com. Online browsing can be tracked because every time a user logs on to a computer, they are assigned a different IP address. Each page clicked on is recorded on an activity log linked to that number. After a federal subpoena, Expedia.com pulled up the IP addresses of every person who had looked at a map of West Alton in the previous few days. Investigators found an IP address linked to a user who had clicked on a map of West Alton several times. Microsoft matched this number to a specific user, MSN/maurytravis.

On June 7, 2002 the police searched Travis' home and found blood and physical evidence linking him to the killings, and he was arrested and charged with seven murders. Three days later, and before admitting guilt, he hanged himself in jail.

Solving Crime with Computers

Computer forensics is used to search for, collect, and analyze information on a computer that could be used to solve a crime. In the early days of computers, courts considered computers as a resource for solid evidence. As computers have become more sophisticated, it was discovered that computer evidence can be easy to change, or corrupt. Computer scientists, working together with detectives, developed what is now known as computer forensics, which focuses on securing, recovering, and analyzing data without altering it. This includes recovering deleted data, which is never completely gone. Even after the recycling bin has been emptied, the

In Switzerland and Germany, facial recognition technology is already being used. This system is able to compare facial features in a database from video images.

computer notes that the space that occupied that file is still available and will remain there until it is overwritten. With certain software, deleted files that have not yet been overwritten can be retrieved.

High-tech programs available to law enforcement today are targeting many specific tasks. There is software to analyze bloodstain patterns found at crime scenes. Advances in ballistics analysis have enabled the use of 3-D computer technology, which helps figure out where the gun was fired. The use of digital surveillance for XBox (XFT Device) was developed after criminals discovered that the gaming system was a good place to hide computer data.

Facial identification software contains images and biographical information about criminals from across the United States. Computer forensic investigators also use 3-D forensic facial reconstruction software to create a possible physical appearance from real human remains.

DNA analysis is still the primary focus of forensic scientists, and one of the newest technologies available is called the Snapshot DNA Phenotyping Service. This computer program uses DNA to create a physical profile by determining how genetic information is translated into physical characteristics. Snapshot reads thousands of genotypes, or genetic differences from a DNA sample, and uses the data to predict what the person looks like. It can accurately predict eye and hair color, ancestry, and even freckling and face shape.

The Fingerprint Database

The FBI's Integrated Automated Fingerprint Identification System (IAFIS) is another example of technology that is making a significant difference to task forces and other law enforcement personnel throughout the country. Established in 1999, this national fingerprint and criminal history database is the largest in the world and contains more than 59 million criminal records. In using it, even the smallest law enforcement agency can have access to the prints of felons throughout the United States, which is an opportunity they did not have with earlier paper systems.

When a task force wants to identify an unknown fingerprint, it scans it electronically and enters it into the IAFIS. There, it is digitally encoded into a geometric pattern. It is then compared to other prints in the system previously submitted by local, state, and federal law enforcement agencies throughout the country. The program comes up with prints that are possible matches, and investigators then make a final point-by-point visual comparison of the unknown print with the alternatives. On TV, fingerprint results are typically discovered instantly; in reality, the process takes about two hours. This is still significantly faster than the old process, where the unknown print had to be manually compared to the thousands of prints that an agency had in its paper files.

By the Numbers

350,653

number of investigations that CODIS has assisted in as of 2017

A Forensic Index

In the late 1980s, the realization that DNA could be used to tie criminals to their crimes motivated law enforcement agencies to begin compiling databases similar in ideology to IAFIS. In 1990, the FBI created the Combined DNA Index System (CODIS), which tied together 14 local and state DNA laboratories in an information-sharing service. In 1998, CODIS was expanded to include the federal government's National DNA Index System, and participating labs soon existed in all 50 states plus the District of Columbia and Puerto Rico.

CODIS consists of a forensic index containing DNA evidence found at crime scenes and an offender index, which holds the DNA profiles of known offenders of sex offenses and other violent crimes. Those profiles are created from blood drawn from an offender and processed in the lab. Forensic labs throughout the United States regularly electronically exchange and compare DNA profiles through CODIS, and as of 2017, more than 365,634 hits have been made, linking unknown DNA to known offenders.

Some CODIS hits have involved serial killers. In 2004, Alexander Wayne Watson Jr. was identified as the murderer of at least three women in Maryland between 1986 and 1993. Police found saliva on an unlit cigarette near one of the bodies, submitted the DNA found on it to CODIS, and were given Watson's name. California's CODIS connected Chester Dewayne Turner to 13 murders that occurred in Los Angeles between 1987 and 1998 after he was found guilty of sexually assaulting a woman in 2002. In 2007, he was sentenced to death in the killing of 10 women. Dianna Bright, the younger sister of one of the victims, said upon his sentencing, "You think that you've gotten over the death, and then you get that call that tells you that you've got to come to court and everything's starting over again. It's like a wound that's scratched up again. Now all of us have a chance to heal ... We can breathe and move on."[40]

Criminal Databases

In addition to IAFIS and CODIS, computerized information systems are also available to make connections between the thousands of facts gathered in serial-killing cases. Once technicians input such data, the computer can collect it in a variety of ways with just the click of a mouse. Thousands of files are scanned in a matter of minutes, allowing task force members to look for cases where the killer drives a white car, uses a knife as a weapon, and poses the body, for instance, or for cases where the killer operates only in one particular state and cuts the buttons off victims' clothes after he kills them. One of these systems is the Washington State Homicide Investigation Tracking System (HITS). HITS was developed in 1987 by Bob LaMoria, Robert D. Keppel, and Joseph Weis of the University of Washington. It allows investigators to choose from as many as 250 fields of information, ranging from geographic location of the crimes to absence or presence of clothing on the bodies.

Washington is not the only state to have its own crime database. Florida has the FALCON Integrated Criminal History System. New York City has its Real Time Crime Center, made up of several computer databases that are accessed centrally to quickly relay information and analysis to detectives in the field. Illinois has the Citizen Law Enforcement Analysis and Reporting system (CLEAR). CLEAR includes an Automated Arrest Application that electronically processes arrests, has Mobile Identification Devices that collect fingerprints and photographs of criminals, and Portable Data Terminals which provide high-speed, wireless access to CLEAR records. In Chicago, within the first 4 years of the program, average crime rates dropped about 6 percent. Agencies in Wisconsin and Indiana and many federal agencies used CLEAR as a model, plus it is the foundation of I-CLEAR, a statewide system featuring interactive maps, community crime alerts, and wanted persons notices.

Nationwide Criminal Data Information

The FBI's National Crime Information Center (NCIC), headquartered in Clarksburg, West Virginia, provides an index of criminal information at no charge to those who wish to use it. Established in 1967, the NCIC started out with five files and 356,784 records. By 2015, it had 21 files and 12 million active records.

A Closer Look at a
Computer Forensics Investigator

Job Description:
The computer forensics investigator fights cybercrime and assists in other investigations to track, locate, and retrieve digital information that could provide evidence to solve crimes.

Education:
A computer forensics investigator needs a bachelor's degree in criminal justice, computer forensics, or computer science. Additionally, the Certified Forensics Computer Examiner (CFEC) certification from the Association of Computer Investigative Specialists may also be helpful. A license, such as a private investigator license, may be required in some states.

Personal Qualifications:
Computer forensics investigators must be able to work independently but should be able to communicate well with the other members of the investigative team. They must have good problem-solving skills, patience, and resourcefulness. They must have full knowledge of applicable computer systems and stay up to date on new technologies. They also must have an understanding of the criminal justice system.

Salary:
The median annual salary of a computer forensics investigator in the United States in 2016 was $68,357.

The database includes information regarding fugitives with active arrest warrants, parolees, missing persons, and unidentified human remains, as well as firearms records and driver's license information. Designed to complement metropolitan and statewide systems, the NCIC is used by thousands of agencies, including federal, state, local, and tribal law enforcement authorities; members of the U.S. intelligence community; and foreign agencies such as the Royal Canadian Mounted Police. Glenn Woods emphasizes that data-sharing systems are the key to catching today's highly mobile criminal: "If you have murders in Los Angeles, Reno, New York City and El Paso, unless these jurisdictions are entering the cases into a central system, they may never be recognized as being linked to the same offender."[41]

New technologies are being developed all the time to help law enforcement agencies such as the FBI solve serial killings and other violent crimes.

The FBI's Violent Criminal Apprehension Program (ViCAP) is a nationwide data information center specific to murder, sexual assaults, missing persons, and unidentified remains. Its creator, former Los Angeles detective Pierce Brooks, helped design it to "provide all law enforcement agencies reporting similar-pattern violent crimes with the information necessary to initiate a coordinated multiagency investigation."[42] When crimes—solved, unsolved, or only attempted—are committed anywhere in the United States, information can be submitted to ViCAP and logged into its system. Investigators who are looking for crimes similar to those in their region can then access the system, focus on a particular method of operating or signature, and perhaps discover that a murder in Los Angeles is linked to one committed in Seattle. Colonel J.R. Burton of the Hillsborough County Sheriff's Office in Florida, who is the former chairman of the ViCAP National Advisory Board, said, "ViCAP gives local and state investigators real advantages—direct access to a national database, analytical support to help identify a suspect, and connectivity to the cases of law enforcement agencies nationwide."[43]

The most notorious serial killer to be apprehended with the help of ViCAP was the Railroad Killer, Ángel Maturino Reséndiz, who took the lives of 15 people in Kentucky, Illinois, and Texas between 1986 and 1999. Reséndiz's victims all lived near the railroads he continuously rode throughout the United States, Mexico, and Canada. The unauthorized immigrant and convicted felon was not immediately suspected in most of the killings, but when information was entered into ViCAP, his name popped up. Authorities apprehended him in July 1999, when he surrendered in El Paso, Texas.

By the Numbers

17,492,427

the record number of transactions processed by the NCIC in a single day

"Quite a Chore"

Even though computers and information technology help law enforcement officials track serial killers, the systems are not perfect and remain a supplement to traditional police methods. Asking questions and getting statements from people are still valuable in a police investigation. Some of the technological weaknesses stem from the fact that the databases are incomplete. Not all police departments take the time to input their information. Some report information inaccurately or irregularly.

A study done by the Office of Technology Assessment (OTA) revealed that about "25.7 percent of the records sent by the FBI's identification division were 'complete, accurate, and unambiguous.'"[44] About 46 percent of NCIC's records held these standards. Incorrect data can result from data entry mistakes, sloppy data collection, or misinterpretation

Other High-Tech Tactics

The National Integrated Ballistic Information Network (NIBIN) is another national database that allows bullets and cartridges recovered from a crime scene to be compared with other bullets and cartridges from prior crime scenes. This system is available in more than 75 locations.

High-tech tactics are not limited to computers. In 2012, an invention was created called the LABRADOR (Light-weight Analyzer for Buried Remains and Decomposition Odor Recognition). The device is used to "sniff out" 30 classes of chemicals that are emitted from decaying bodies and is useful in missing persons cases. In 2011, physicists Christopher Varney and Fred Gittes at Washington State University used trigonometry to analyze blood spatter patterns to determine the position of the source of the blood spatter.

Laser Ablation Inductively Coupled Plasma Mass Spectrometry (LA-ICP-MS) is an analytical technique used to examine tiny bits of glass and break them down to their atomic structure. This way, even the most trace amounts of glass shards found on clothing can be connected to a glass sample from a crime scene.

of the information. Another study by the OTA showed that federal agencies rarely audit the quality of the data and that they have low standards for accuracy.

When ViCAP was rolled out in 1985, the late senator Arlen Specter wrote that "[ViCAP'S] implementation could mean the prevention of countless murders and the prompt apprehension of violent criminals."[45] However, ViCAP never really delivered. As of 2015, only 1,400 police agencies in the United States out of 18,000 participate in the system. The database receives reports on less than 1 percent of violent crimes committed each year. A review in the 1990s showed that the system had linked only 33 crimes in 12 years. Staffing and training of ViCAP program staff has been cut dramatically. Local police find the system time-consuming and difficult to use, with false positives a common occurrence. According to Phoenix police department criminal analyst Jeff Jensen, "We don't really use ViCAP … It really is quite a chore."[46]

In the Wrong Hands

Technology is useful, but when it is in the wrong hands it can be terrifying. Just as police and investigative work have improved with technology, so have the murderous tactics of some serial killers. Social media has been

The Canadian Violent Criminal Linkage Analysis System

Soon after ViCAP was created, Canadian law enforcement officials used it as a model to develop their own system called the Violent Criminal Linkage Analysis System (ViCLAS). Unlike the United States, Canada's program is well staffed and well funded, and unlike the United States, reporting to the system is mandatory. The Royal Canadian Mounted Police said the database contains more than 500,000 criminal case profiles as opposed to the FBI, which has about 89,000 cases on file. The agency also claims that it has linked more than 7,000 unsolved crimes since 1995. If the FBI collected information as often as the Canadian police, based on the United States population, its database would have more than 4.4 million cases.

Police using the ViCLAS system have similar complaints as U.S. law enforcement, such as that the system is timely and complicated, but according to Sergeant Tony Lawlor, who is a senior ViCLAS analyst, "it has information which assists police officers, which is catching bad guys ... When police realize there's a value associated with it, they use it."[1]

1. Quoted in T. Christian Miller, "Why Can't the FBI Identify Serial Rapists?," *The Atlantic*, July 30, 2015, www.theatlantic.com/politics/archive/2015/07/vicap-fbi-database/399986/.

a particularly effective way for serial killers to attract their victims. No longer does the killer have to search the streets, waiting for his opportunity, when the Internet makes meeting people so easy.

John Edward Robinson is generally known as the Internet's first serial killer. Robinson discovered the Internet in the mid-1990s and searched social networking sites for women who were willing to engage in sexual activity with him. Two of the women also thought that he was offering them jobs and agreed to get together with him because they were desperate for money and were never seen again. A missing person's report filed on one of the victims led the police to Robinson's farm in Kansas, where the bodies of Suzette Trouten and Izabela Lewicka were found in 85-pound (38.5 kg) chemical drums. He was also responsible for killing three other women and is currently on death row.

The Long Island Serial Killer, still at large, used Craigslist to find sex workers before he killed them and dumped their remains on Gilgo Beach. Stephen Port, the Grindr Killer, found his male victims on dating websites and invited them to his apartment. After arriving, Port would give the men drinks spiked with drugs in doses large enough to kill them. While they were unconscious, he would rape them.

Serial killings may be on the decline, but the accessibility of the Internet and dozens of social media sites makes it much easier for killers to hunt their prey. The best way to catch these murderers is to combine as many resources as possible and work as a team. It is also important, now more than ever, for law enforcement to use every resource they have—from profiling techniques, to the analysis of a crime scene, to the most high-tech investigative gadgets available—when they are tracking serial killers.

Notes

Introduction: The Killers Next Door

1. Quoted in "Rader Used Scouts as a Ruse in Final Murder," *The Witchita Eagle*, August 17, 2005. www.kansas.com/news/special-reports/btk/article1003773.html.

2. Jason Kravarik, "Who Is Dennis Rader?," KSN.com, February 26, 2005. www.freerepublic.com/focus/news/1351569/replies?c=565.

Chapter One: Serial Killer Task Force

3. "Serial Killers Part 8: New Research Aims to Help Investigators Solve Cases," FBI.gov, October 10, 2014. www.fbi.gov/news/stories/serial-killers-part-8-new-research-aims-to-help-investigators-solve-serial-murder-cases.

4. John Philpin, "To Catch a Killer: A Field Guide to the Baton Rouge Serial Murder Investigation," KariSable.com, 2003. www.karisable.com/skazbr2.htm.

5. Leonard Ortiz, "Inside the Task Force Hunting a Serial Killer," *Orange County Register*, January 12, 2012. www.ocregister.com/articles/wyatt-335359-force-task.html.

6. Ann Rule, *Green River, Running Red: The Real Story of The Green River Killer—America's Deadliest Serial Murderer*. New York, NY: Pocket Star Books, 2004, p. 328.

7. "Ex-policeman Nicknamed 'Werewolf' Confesses to Murdering 24 Women in Siberia," *The Siberian Times*, November 6, 2013. www.siberiantimes.com/other/others/features/ex-policeman-nicknamed-werewolf-confesses-to-murdering-24-women-in-siberia.

8. Mike Barber, "Part 4: Serial Killers Prey on 'the Less Dead,'" *Seattle PI*, February 19, 2003. www.seattlepi.com/news/article/Part-4-Serial-killers-prey-on-the-less-dead-1107551.php.

9. Sandi Doughton, "Why Did Ridgway Do It? Experts Say He's Like Other Serial Killers," *The Seattle Times*, November 10, 2003. old.seattletimes.com/html/greenriverkillings/2001787301_ridgmind10m.html.

10. Quoted in Alex Tsakiris, "Pyschic Detectives and Police," Skeptiko, November 23. www.skeptiko.com/58-psychic-detectives-and-police.

11. Sarah Kernshaw, "21-Year Hunt for Killer Shapes Man and Family," *New York Times*, November 7, 2003. www.nytimes.com/2003/11/07/us/21-year-hunt-for-killer-shapes-man-and-family.html.

Chapter Two: Profiling

12. Arnon Edelstein, "Serial Murder Profiling: Our Contemporary Understanding," *Journal of Forensic Medicine and Legal Affairs*, July 25, 2016, 1(2): 111. www.elynsgroup.com/journal/article/serial-murder-profiling-our-contemporary-understanding.

13. Shanna Freeman, "How Serial Killers Work," HowStuffWorks, accessed April 26, 2017. people.howstuffworks.com/serial-killer6.htm.

14. Natasha Mitchell, "In the Mind of the Psychopath," ABC.net, March 24, 2002. www.abc.net.au/radionational/programs/allinthemind/in-the-mind-of-the-sychopath/3506864#transcript.

15. Robert D. Keppel and William J. Birnes, *Signature Killers*. New York, NY: Pocket Books, 1997, pp. 26–27.

16. Quoted in Burl Barer, *Body Count*. New York, NY: Pinnacle Books, 2002, e-book.

17. Quoted in Becky Sullivan, "All Things Considered," NPR, December 29, 2013. www.npr.org/2013/12/29/258160192/the-fbi-investigator-who-coined-the-term-serial-killer.

Chapter Three: Public Attention

18. Bill Morlin and Jeanette White, *Bad Trick: The Hunt for Spokane's Serial Killer*, Spokane, WA: New Media Ventures, Inc., 2001, p. 130.

19. Dirk Cameron Gibson, *Serial Murder and Media Circuses*, Westport, CT: Praeger, 2006, p. 170.

20. Christine Pelisek, "Long Island Serial Killer: How Close are Police to Catching the Suspect—or Suspects?," *People*, November 3, 2016. www.people.com/crime/long-island-serial-killer-update-police-fbi-investigation.

21. Katherine Ramsland, "Too Easy to Criticize a Difficult Manhunt," *Philadelphia Inquirer*, June 3, 2003.

22. Mark Fuhrman, *Murder in Spokane: Catching a Serial Killer*. New York, NY: Cliff Street Books, 2001, p. 291.

23. "David Kaczynski Speaks on the Death Penalty," Colorado Law, April 7, 2006. lawweb.colorado.edu/news/showArticle.jsp?id=201.

24. Robert Beattie, *Nightmare in Wichita*, New York, NY: New American Library, 2005, p. 321.

25. Morlin and White, *Bad Trick: The Hunt for Spokane's Serial Killer*, p. 74.

26. Roy Wenzl, "DNA of Retired Police Sought in BTK Probe," *The Witchita Eagle*, November 21, 2004. www.kansas.com/news/special-reports/btk/article1003611.html.

27. Stanley Crouch, "US Is Still Land of Law and Order," Booker Rising, October 30, 2005. bookerrising.blogspot.com/2005_10_01_bookerrising_archive.html.

Chapter Four: The Crime Lab

28. Quoted in PerkinElmer, "Moving IR Spectroscopy Down to the Micron Level Puts Serial Killer Behind Bars," 2005. www.perkinelmer.com/CMSResources/Images/44-74514CST_murderconviction.pdf.

29. Morlin and White, *Bad Trick: The Hunt for Spokane's Serial Killer*, p. 42.

30. Bill Morlin and Jeannette White, "Crawling with Cops—Detectives Begin Search of Robert Yates' Home, but the Best Evidence Would Come from a Lab," Spokane (WA) Spokesman-Review, July 27, 2001, p. B1.

31. Henry C. Lee, Timothy Palmbach, and Marilyn T. Miller, *Henry Lee's Crime Scene Handbook*. San Diego, CA: Elsevier Academic Press, 2001, p. 135.

32. Barer, *Body Count*, pp. 228–229.

33. Shannon Rasp, "Taking a Bite Out of Crime: Forensic Dentistry," *HealthLEADER*, October 29, 2010. www.uthealthleader.org/story/taking-a-bite-out-of-crime.

34. Rasp, "Taking a Bite Out of Crime: Forensic Dentistry."

35. Fernanda Santos, "Evidence from Bite Marks, It Turns Out, Is Not So Elementary," *New York Times*, January 28, 2007. www.nytimes.com/2007/01/28/weekinreview/28santos.html.

36. Katherine Ramsland, "The Most Famous Bite," Crime Library, 2006. www.crimelibrary.com/forensics/bitemarks.

37. Katherine Ramsland, "Identification," Crime Library, 2006. www.crimelibrary.com/criminal_mind/forensics/anthropology/2.html?sect=21.

38. Richard Roth, "How Do Serial Killer Suspects Elude Police?" CNN, June 24, 1999. www.cnn.com/US/9906/24/serial.mo.

Chapter Five:
Forensic Technology

39. Stephanie Simon, "Virtual Trail Led to Serial Killer Suspect," *Los Angeles Times*. June 17, 2002. articles.latimes.com/2002/jun/17/nation/na-serial17.

40. Jack Leonard, "Jury Decides Death for Convicted Serial Killer Chester Dewayne Turner," *Los Angeles Times*, June 26, 2014. www.latimes.com/local/la-me-chester-turner-penalty-20140627-story.html.

41. Bill McGarigle, "Crime Profilers Gain New Weapons," Government Technology, November 30, 1997. www.govtech.com/magazines/gt/Crime-Profilers-Gain-New-Weapons.html.

42. Criminal Profiling Staff, "The New ViCAP," Criminal Profiling, February 18, 2005. www.criminalprofiling.com/The-New-ViCAP_s319.html.

43. Federal Bureau of Investigation, "ViCAP, Fighting Violent Crime for 25 Years," FBI.gov, August 10, 2010. archives.fbi.gov/archives/news/stories/2010/august/vicap-anniversary.

44. Michael McFarland, "The Human Cost of Computer Errors," Santa Clara University, June 1, 2012. www.scu.edu/ethics/focus-areas/internet-ethics/resources/the-human-cost-of-computer-errors/.

45. T. Christian Miller, "Why Can't the FBI Identify Serial Rapists?," *The Atlantic*, July 30, 2015, www.theatlantic.com/politics/archive/2015/07/vicap-fbi-database/399986/.

46. Miller, "Why Can't the FBI Identify Serial Rapists?"

For More Information

Books

Fraser, Jim. *Forensic Science: A Very Quick Introduction*. Oxford, UK: OUP Oxford, 2010.
This book gives a basic explanation of forensic science as it applies to a crime scene.

Newton, Michael. *The Encyclopedia of Serial Killers*. New York, NY: Checkmark Books, 2006.
This book is an extensive reference concerning the case histories of several serial killers.

Philbin, Tom, and Michael Philbin. *The Killer Book of Serial Killers: Incredible Stories, Facts, and Trivia from the World of Serial Killers*. Naperville, IL: Sourcebooks, 2009.
This book features stories, odd facts, and trivia about serial killers.

Rule, Ann. *Green River, Running Red: The Real Story of The Green River Killer—America's Deadliest Serial Murderer*. New York, NY: Pocket Star Books, 2004.
In this book, Ann Rule writes about her 20 years of research on the Green River Killer.

Wilson, Colin. *Serial Killer Investigations: The Story of Forensics and Profiling Through the Hunt for the World's Worst Murderers*. Chichester, UK: Summersdale Publishers, 2007.
This book gives a closer look at psychological profiling, fingerprinting, and forensics in general.

Websites

Computer Forensics Training 101
(www.computerforensics
training101.com/class-course.
html)
This website explores the world
of computer forensics, including training and education.

Crime Museum
(www.crimemuseum.org/
crime-library/serial-killers/)
This website includes a list of
links with details about specific serial killers.

FBI
(www.fbi.gov/stats-services/
publications/serial-murder)
The official FBI website gives
an in-depth look into how the
organization investigates
serial murders.

"How Forensic Lab
Techniques Work"
(science.howstuffworks.com/
forensic-lab-technique.htm)
This article provides useful
information on forensic lab
techniques used in
murder investigations.

"The Making of a Serial Killer"
(www.psychologytoday.
com/blog/the-superhuman-
mind/201212/the-making-
serial-killer)
This article gives insight into
what causes a serial killer to
do what they do.

Index

Picture Credits

Cover Couperfield/Shutterstock.com; p. 7 Pool/Pool/Getty Images News/Getty Images; p. 8 Chicago History Museum/Contributor/Archive Photos/Getty Images; pp. 12, 25, 40, 49, 58 Bettmann/Contributor/Bettmann/Getty Images; p. 15 REUTERS/Alamy Stock Photo; p. 17 AkeSak/Shutterstock.com; p. 19 Jack the Ripper: Metropolitan Police poster of 3 October 1888 (litho), English School (19th century)/Private Collection/Peter Newark Historical Pictures/Bridgeman Images; p. 24 Ron Bull/Contributor/Toronto Star/Getty Images; p. 26 SHAWN THEW/Stringer/AFP/Getty Images; p. 29 Fairfx Media/Contributor/Fairfax Media/ Getty Images; p. 34 Curt Borgwardt/Contributor/Sygma/Getty Images; p. 35 AP Photo/Rachel D'Oro; p. 37 AP Photo; p. 45 Rex Features via AP Images; p. 46 Tim Boyle/Contributor/Hulton Archive/Getty Images; p. 51 Handout/Handout/ Getty Images Entertainment/Getty Images; p. 56 AP Photo/David J. Phillip, POOL; p. 60 ZUMA Press, Inc./Alamy Stock Photo; p. 64 M Phillips David/Science Source/Getty Images; p. 67 Paul Taylor/Corbis/Getty Images; p. 69 revers/ Shutterstock.com; p. 72 Konstantin Faraktinov/Shutterstock.com; p. 76 CRISTINA QUICLER/Stringer/AFP/Getty Images; p. 79 Heroc/Shutterstock.com; p. 84 South_ agency/E+/Getty Images.

About the Author

Christine Honders lives in upstate New York with her husband, Rob, and her three children, Marcus, Juliet, and Jamie. She has written more than 20 books for elementary and middle school readers, including *Bloodsucking Birds* and *Ancient Maya Culture*. She also enjoys singing and performing with different local musicians.